Preparing Students for
Testing
and
Doing Better
in School

To the memory of my father, Theodore G. Fleig. You were a great student, and you will always be loved and remembered.

To my father-in-law, Asher J. Fox, who pursued knowledge for the sheer joy of knowing and articulating ideas. We miss you so very much.

And to our granddaughters, Elena Graham, a kindergarten graduate and now in first grade, and Zoe Graham, our littlest one, in four-year-old kindergarten. Both of you are the joys of Grandma's and Papa's (Grandpa's) lives. We are proud of how prepared you are for doing well in school: you are both so interested in reading and studying books, and we observe how you create and develop new ideas and learning all the time. We love you so!

Elena studying her new book

Zoe playing a learning/relationship game with author (Grandma)

Photos by Tyler Fox (Papa), Elena's and Zoe's Grandpa

Preparing Students for
Testing
and
Doing Better
in School

Rona F. Flippo
Foreword by P. David Pearson

Skyhorse Publishing

Skyhorse Publishing books may be purchased in bulk at special discounts for sales promotion, corporate gifts, fund-raising, or educational purposes. Special editions can also be created to specifications. For details, contact the Special Sales Department, Skyhorse Publishing, 307 West 36th Street, 11th Floor, New York, NY 10018 or info@skyhorsepublishing.com.

Skyhorse® and Skyhorse Publishing® are registered trademarks of Skyhorse Publishing, Inc.®, a Delaware corporation.

Visit our website at www.skyhorsepublishing.com.

10 9 8 7 6 5 4 3 2 1

Library of Congress Cataloging-in-Publication Data is available on file.

Cover design by Monique Hahn

Print ISBN: 978-1-62914-721-5
Ebook ISBN: 978-1-63220-095-2

Printed in the China

Contents

Foreword

Rona Flippo has done it again—given teachers and students a wonderful gift in the form of a book that demystifies this phenomenon we call testing! The gift is even more special than the earlier versions of guides of this type she has prepared. Why? Because we live in a world in which tests exert entirely too much influence (some for the good but most for the bad) on students and their teachers. Rona's book will do much to help students and their teachers exert authority over the tests rather than vice versa.

The guide is neatly organized into three parts, each an important piece of the puzzle one has to solve to become a master over rather than a slave to tests. Part One, not surprisingly, emphasizes what teachers, and by implication their students, can do *throughout the school year* to get ready for tests. Within Part One is lots of good advice about how to help students get themselves organized both *as students* and *as learners*. The suggestions here have to do with budgeting time, looking ahead to determine deadlines and periods that are likely to induce lots of pressure to get things done, planning ahead for those pressure periods, and the like. Part Two gets closer to the tests themselves and details, in great and useful detail, strategies for teachers to use to get their students into the right frame of mind in the days leading up to a test. These chapters contain lots of good advice about general skills and, more importantly, how to align study strategies to the test's format. She makes an important distinction between tests that emphasize "bite-size" pieces, such as multiple-choice, completion, and matching, and those that emphasize "big ideas" and synthesizing them in relevant ways, namely essay tests. To complete the cycle, Part Three discusses strategies for students to use when they are in the throes of actually taking the test.

In terms of features, teachers and students will find Appendix B an especially useful resource because the activities included will allow students to "practice" becoming test-wise before it counts for real. And the Web resources in Appendix A will appeal to this generation of tech-savvy students (even though the information in the book is more useful and relevant!).

I really like this three-part structure because I don't think a student can be truly effective until and unless all three of these sets of strategies (being a good student, getting ready by studying, and being an effective test taker) are in place. If we emphasize one to the exclusion of the other two, we will leave students vulnerable to unforeseen circumstances. But my favorite part is the chapter on taking essay tests. What is so refreshing about

Flippo's treatment of how to take an essay test is her emphasis on what students should do *before* they set pen to paper (or fingers to keyboard) and what they should do *after* they think they are finished. All too many students write themselves into corners and cul-de-sacs that they cannot easily escape if they rush into writing down their answers. And even more students budget no time to review what they have written to see if it passes the "Does this make sense and is it responsive to the task?" test. As a result, they don't show their best stuff and suffer accordingly in grades or scores.

I cannot tell you how refreshing it is to see such brevity and clarity in a book that must appeal to both teachers and students. It is a meaty treatment of the vexing world of taking tests. But Flippo gets right to the point and does not take us down misleading side roads or detours. If this is meat, it is all lean and muscle without a lot of excess fat. We should all be grateful that Professor Flippo cares as much as she does about the plight of students and the goals of teachers committed to helping them become the type of students they would like to be. Happy reading (I will resist the temptation to say, Happy test taking)!

P. David Pearson
Dean of the Graduate School of Education
University of California–Berkeley

Acknowledgments

Over the years, many students, teachers, and college professors have used earlier editions of my test preparation materials. These have been middle school, high school, and college students who needed to learn important study and test-taking techniques as well as their teachers who wanted to learn how to help students develop these strategies. These students became better prepared, their teachers became more confident, and I became even more convinced that study and test-preparation strategies can be both learned and developed and, as a result, students could learn how to do better in school. Thank you all for what you have taught me.

My graduate student, Amy MacDougall, at the University of Massachusetts Boston, deserves very special recognition for her work on this current book. Amy thoroughly reviewed the material and made very important contributions to this new work. Thank you, Amy, for your feedback, research, development of new exercises, and assistance throughout the development of this book. They were invaluable to me.

Dari-Ann D. Holland, an accomplished special educator with the Boston Public Schools in Massachusetts and my exceptional former graduate student at the University of Massachusetts Boston, came to my rescue and took over many author responsibilities during the production phases of this book. As my valued colleague and assistant, Dari-Ann dealt with editorial queries, the copyedited manuscript, reference research, and the various issues arising during page proofing. Dari-Ann, thank you from the bottom of my heart for your very professional contributions and know-how.

Marilyn J. Becker, Director of Learner Development at the University of Minnesota Medical School and a licensed psychologist who provides support in areas including learning and test performance, is specially acknowledged for her expertise and assistance with *Preparing Students for Testing and Doing Better in School*. Her review, suggestions, and affirmation of the material in this book have been of great value and importance.

Jessica Myers, librarian, consultant to a large Boston museum library, specialist in technical services, and graduate of the Simmons Graduate School of Library and Information Science in Boston, is thanked for her contributions to this material.

P. David Pearson, noted educator, scholar, and Dean of the Graduate School of Education at the University of California–Berkeley, merits a big thank-you as acknowledgment for his contribution. David, I value your endorsement of this book. Your opinion means a lot to me. Thank you for your thoughtful review and for authoring the Foreword.

Ron Elbert, my skilled typist and editor, as always deserves special recognition. Thank you, Ron, for all you do to make everything "work." You are invaluable to me as well.

Tyler Fox, my wonderful husband, thank you for taking the great pictures included on the Dedication page of this book of our granddaughters, Elena and Zoe, as they study and learn.

It would be remiss not to include an honorary acknowledgment of Alton Raygor, who was Professor Emeritus of Educational Psychology at the University of Minnesota and my reviewer and collaborator for the first edition of my first book in this area, *TestWise* (1988). Al, I miss you, and I have not forgotten all that I learned from you.

And finally, thank you to my husband (Tyler Fox), my daughter (Tara Flippo), and my granddaughters (Elena Graham and Zoe Graham), whose constant love and support have sustained me throughout the completion of this material.

We gratefully acknowledge the contributions of the following professionals and reviewers:

Rosalie Fink, EdD
Professor of Literacy
Lesley University
Cambridge, MA

Richard D. Robinson, EdD
Professor of Education
University of Missouri–Columbia
Columbia, MO

Ed Fry, PhD
Professor Emeritus
Rutgers University
New Brunswick, NJ

Sharon Schulze
Interim Director
The Science House
North Carolina State University
Raleigh, NC

Linda B. Gambrell, PhD
Distinguished Professor of Education
Eugene T. Moore School of
  Education
Clemson University
Clemson, SC

Richard T. Vacca, PhD
Professor Emeritus
Kent State University
Kent, OH

Buck Wall
Department Chair of
  Social Studies
Hillcrest High School
Simpsonville, NC

Tricia Peña
Principal
Cienega High School
Vail, AZ

About the Author

 **Rona F. Flippo, EdD,** has taught in public schools and has been a professor of reading and study strategy education at various colleges and universities in the United States, including in Florida, South Carolina, Georgia, Wisconsin, and Massachusetts. She is currently Professor of Education at the University of Massachusetts Boston in the Graduate College of Education. Dr. Flippo has been a consultant for Educational Testing Services (ETS) and the Georgia Department of Education. Additionally, she serves on various editorial boards, on the Board of Directors of the College Reading Association (CRA), and on various committees of the International Reading Association (IRA). She has published 13 books in addition to this one and over 90 chapters and articles in prestigious professional books and journals; many of these publications have been on study and test-taking research and strategies. Dr. Flippo has worked extensively with elementary, middle school, high school, community college, and university students and their teachers to develop students' study and test strategies. Thousands of students and teachers have learned how to become *prepared* for tests and for doing better in school under Dr. Flippo's tutelage.

How to Use This Book

This is an easy book to use because it provides teachers and other readers with step-by-step guidance for helping students learn what is needed to be successful on tests and in school, from the first day of the school term right through test day. Along the way, *Preparing Students for Testing and Doing Better in School* provides plenty of opportunities for students to practice using the tools and strategies that will help them get better test scores and ultimately do better in school.

This book divides the process of becoming prepared and doing better in school into three parts:

1. How to get students organized and in the right frame of mind to study, learn, and take tests

2. How to study for essay and objective tests

3. How to answer and take essay and objective questions and tests

Some of the chapters present general *preparing students* skills, and others present specific strategies for essay and objective questions and tests. You (the teacher, other professional, or parent using this book) should work through the exercises in the entire book with your student(s). Supplement them, as you see fit, with your own materials that they must study. Give your students as much opportunity as possible to practice for their upcoming tests.

All students should have an opportunity to read or be exposed to the information in Part One. Chapter 1 describes how to avoid test panic. It provides advice and techniques for psyching up, relaxing before and during tests, and making course notes and readings useful study resources. In Chapter 2, students will learn how to plan for their tests each term. This chapter explains how to make a master schedule for all tests, how to anticipate what each test will contain, and how to schedule test-study time.

Part Two is about studying for tests. In Chapter 3 are general test-study techniques and strategies. Students will learn how to make study notes and how to memorize them as well as the right way to do a final cram before a test. Chapter 4 is about studying for essay tests—predicting various kinds of essay questions and practicing answers to them. Chapter 5 covers study strategies for the various kinds of objective questions—multiple-choice, matching, true/false, and completion.

Part Three gives information and practice opportunities so students will learn how to take tests. Chapter 6 contains advice for getting ready on exam day so students can focus all their energy on doing well on the test. In Chapter 7, students will learn how to budget their time to take an essay test and how to write essay answers that are complete, clear, and to the point. Taking objective tests is the subject of Chapter 8. There, students will learn how to pace themselves so they will have time to come back to questions that stumped them the first time around. And when needed, students will learn the clues to look for in multiple-choice, matching, true/false, and completion questions to help them identify the right answers.

If your students are preparing specifically for an essay test, they can skip Chapters 5 and 8. If they are about to take an objective test, Chapters 4 and 7 won't be necessary right now. But to become completely *prepared*, students should work through the exercises you assign throughout the book. And after they have worked all the way through the exercises selected or adapted in *Preparing Students,* they should keep them as a reference and return to those—relaxation techniques or the cues for multiple-choice questions, for example—that will help them prepare for future tests.

So that students can stay *prepared*, reproducible blank copies of the test-preparation and test-study tools—including study schedules and the test analysis form—are provided in Appendix B of this book. Copy them and use them with your students! Additionally, you will find in Appendix C an up-to-date listing of Web sites and other resources that provide additional test-preparation assistance, should you wish to use it. There are also many jargon and testing terms used throughout the book that you, your students, and their families should be aware of, and these are included in a glossary in Appendix D.

One last word about *Preparing Students:* This book is designed especially for *all* teacher-made and departmental tests. Even though most of the information here will help students with standardized tests, it is recommended that they refer additionally to the study manual(s) for the particular standardized test they are planning to take. Special study guides for the SAT, GED, ACT, CLEP, GRE, and other standardized tests are available from bookstores and libraries. Because each of these study guides usually provides sample practice questions that parallel the particular test, and other specific and important details concerning the standardized test being taken, your students should have those guides available for perusal. However, the materials you will use with your students in this book cover *all* the basics and all the bases of good test preparation and test taking; they should do well both to prepare your students for *all* tests and help them do better in school.

No matter what kind of test your students are facing right now, you owe it to them to help them be *prepared* for both essay and objective tests. This book contains the most useful, up-to-date, and accurate information to help you do that.

Note to the Teacher

This book has been developed to meet the needs of both teachers and students. It has been designed for use by teachers of students in grades 6 through high school, but even students new to the rigors of college study could benefit. It is for those students who are in middle school and getting ready to meet the demands of high school, for those who are already in high school and would benefit by learning test preparation and test-taking strategies, and for those preparing for college studies and the act of balancing the many required study assignments and tests.

Middle school, high school, and college prep teachers can assign the "Test Prep" exercises from this book and adapt them to fit their own curricula to help students prepare for the specific tests given in their courses. They work well with all content area courses. If you wish, each student could have his or her own copy of this book and be encouraged to work through it, or you can just as easily use the book with the practice exercises and forms provided to teach learning and test-taking strategies to your students. Today, both students and teachers are challenged with mandated high-stakes tests. This book will help you and your students rise to that challenge.

In Appendix D at the end of this book is a glossary of terms. However, all test preparation and test-taking terms are also explained, with many examples, in the text itself. A list of Web sites and books for additional test-preparation assistance can be found in Appendix C. This Appendix should be especially useful for students and their families who want more support and information. In Appendix A, teachers and students will find "Test Prep: The Test," a final exam for students, to allow them to show what they learned from this material about test studying, learning, preparation, test taking, and doing better in school. However, the real learning will be evident to you as your students show you that they are indeed doing better on tests that you give and are more prepared to do better in their school environment.

Another helpful resource to ensure success is Appendix B, which contains the forms and schedules recommended and demonstrated for student use throughout this book. (You may make as many copies of these reproducible forms as you like for practice with your students.)

Teachers can easily adapt the material in this book to meet the needs and curricula of their students. Just supplement some of the text examples provided throughout with examples from your own, more appropriate textbooks. Your students can learn how to learn and succeed in your classroom. There is no need to wait until they are having problems "making the grade" in high school and beyond.

In the current environment of high-stakes testing, the information in this new book, *Preparing Students for Testing and Doing Better in School,* is crucial for all students, teachers, and other school professionals. Congratulations on choosing this material and being proactive for your students' success.

Note to the Student

The material developed for this book has three related purposes—(1) to help you become prepared, (2) to help you do the best you possibly can on every test you take, and (3) to help you do better in school. This is not a book on study skills in general; it is a book with one major idea: *Preparing Students for Testing and Doing Better in School.*

To get the best score possible on a test, it is not enough just to know your subject thoroughly, although that is obviously necessary. You must also know how to prepare for and how to take essay tests and objective tests. This is because a test not only samples your knowledge of a subject, but it also measures your ability to take tests.

To get the best score possible on a test, it is not enough just to go to class, listen, and do the assignments. You must also be able to demonstrate to the teacher that you know the content of the material tested so he or she can evaluate you and give you a grade. The more you can demonstrate what you know, the higher your grade is likely to be. That is the way the system operates.

By being *prepared*, you can make the system work for you. Even if you are not the best student in the class, you will be better *prepared* and feel more confident if you know how to study for and take tests. Being *prepared* is not a gimmick; it means you have the necessary skills to be a better student. The more you know about preparing for and taking tests, and the more you practice the Test Prep exercises and activities in this book with the materials you must learn, the higher your test scores are likely to be. This is what being *prepared* is all about. Likewise, students who have *prepared* themselves adequately will also improve their chances of doing better in school. The preparation and practice materials and the Test Prep exercises that will be assigned from this book are each designed to help you achieve these goals.

Introduction

WHAT DOES IT MEAN TO BE REALLY PREPARED FOR TESTS AND DO BETTER IN SCHOOL?

It means that students know how to play the testing game and come out as winners. It means that students specifically know how to

1. get in the right frame of mind to take a test,

2. use all available resources to study effectively for both objective and essay tests,

3. anticipate the right questions for each test,

4. practice answering those questions before the test,

5. recognize the cues, or clues, given in the test, and

6. use strategies to correctly answer as many questions as possible in the time allotted for the test.

Additionally, test preparation is a good way to study and learn in school. Preparing for tests involves the use and coordination of many study skills, including organization, time management, note taking, and memorization. It also includes the learning and application of specialized strategies for study and learning skills that enable students to prepare for and take essay and objective tests. Test preparation strategies are really good learning strategies as well. Use of these strategies enables many students to do better in school (Flippo, 2002b).

HOW DO STANDARDIZED TESTS FIT IN?

Two up-front but related questions that users of this book are likely to have are "What are standardized tests?" and "How can this book, *Preparing Students for Testing and Doing Better in School*, help students on the standardized tests they must take?" Therefore, before we begin using the *Preparing Students* materials, it is important here to address these questions.

What Are Standardized Tests?

Standardized tests are commercially prepared assessment instruments that are given to those being tested under prescribed and uniform conditions. In 1990, John Pikulski indicated that even though many find fault with standardized tests, it is not likely they will disappear. In fact, he and others, including Sheila Valencia and Karen Wixon (2000), have cited evidence that standardized tests are being used more and for more varied high-stakes purposes than ever. With standardized tests, everyone gets the same test, directions, test information, and time allotment to take the test.

These tests can be further classified as either norm referenced or criterion referenced, referring to how their particular scores have been derived and how these scores will later be reported. Norm-referenced scores are derived by comparing an individual's *raw score* (number of correct answers) to the scores of those in the group on which the test was normed. Therefore, *norm-referenced tests* report the norm-referenced scores of those being tested. Test takers are compared with others who have taken the test. Criterion-referenced scores are test results that have been determined by comparing an individual's raw score to a predetermined passing score for the test or subtest being taken. *Criterion-referenced tests*, then, report whether or not test takers have passed or failed the predetermined criterion of the given test or subtest they have taken. Test takers are not compared to other test takers, just to the criterion.

Consumers of standardized tests often do not realize that norm-referenced tests and criterion-referenced tests can look exactly the same, assess the same objectives and information, and even ask the same questions. This is because the only real difference between them is in how their scores are reported. Those test publishers developing both types of standardized tests build them from specified objectives and then subject them to the necessary procedures either to norm reference them, by first giving the test to others in similar age or grade groups and then using these results to "norm" the test, or to criterion reference them by having knowledgeable persons (for example, experienced experts in the area being tested) review the test questions to determine how many of the answers an individual test taker should be required to get correct to pass the test—thus establishing the "criteria."

Although criticisms of standardized tests and of both types of standardized test scores abound, they tend to concentrate on three major problems and issues. One problem inherent with norm-referenced scored tests is whether the norming groups match those taking the test. A second common complaint, this one against criterion-referenced tests, concerns the arbitrary cut-off scores. A third group of concerns relates to the implications of the high-stakes usage of standardized tests in general. Those who make decisions regarding whether or not to give standardized tests, the extent to which their results will be counted, and which type of standardized test to use must weigh these issues to make informed decisions appropriate for their testing purposes and the populations they will be testing.

Standardized tests and their scores are commonly used as entrance and exit measures for schools, colleges, graduate programs, licensure purposes, and career advancement and other job-related purposes and to evaluate students and schools, colleges, and teachers. Hence their well-known moniker, *high-stakes tests*. The large array of standardized tests often makes it confusing for those making the decisions to select the most appropriate ones. Matching the test to the purpose is thus a very important concern: The technical manuals and other materials accompanying a test must provide full, accurate, and up-to-date information to allow test users to make their decisions. Also important are decisions regarding what should be tested: Should reading, for example, be tested as a product or a process? If it is regarded as a product, questions usually focus on the testing of the more discrete, isolated subskills. The tendency of standardized tests to focus on these skills targets them for criticism by those who believe reading should be treated as a process; in the critics' view, the tests overlook the more important evaluation of students' strategies (Flippo & Schumm, in press).

Special populations of students, for instance those from culturally and linguistically diverse backgrounds and those with particular learning disabilities, are not well served by standardized tests: Making students who come from a non-English-speaking background take tests in English has been highly criticized. Misuse and inappropriate interpretations of standardized test scores are another important issue. Publishers and users of these tests have a grave responsibility to ensure that those in the position to use score information understand it. Technical problems with standardized tests also raise major concerns as to their validity (Flippo, 2002a).

How Can This Book Help Students Prepare for Standardized Tests?

The material in this book is comprehensive and inclusive of all subject areas, and it thoroughly covers the preparation for and the taking of all kinds of tests. What's more, the material in this book has been designed to help students be *prepared* and make the most of the information they have learned in their school subjects and courses. In other words, students using the material contained herein not only develop *test-wise* skills (i.e., knowing how to study and successfully take the various required tests), but also as a result of *being prepared,* they learn more and do better in school. To the extent that a standardized test covers and assesses content that has been learned in school (meaning that the standardized test has *content validity*), students using the *Preparing Students* book should do very well indeed!

In fact, *Preparing Students* provides a thorough grounding in specific strategies for preparing and studying for all types of objective questions in varied content areas (see Chapter 5). These are the types of questions that compose most standardized tests. But if the standardized test your students must take includes essay questions, your students will be ready, because Chapter 4 provides specific strategies for preparing for all types of essay questions across the range of content areas as well. Furthermore, Chapter 8 provides specific strategies to use while actually taking objective tests, while Chapter 7 does the same with essay tests.

PART ONE

Doing Better in School

1

How to Avoid Test Panic

Tests measure students' knowledge of a subject or their ability to perform a skill. Tests are a means for students to show their teachers that they have mastered the course content, and they are a basis for teachers to assign grades. Granted, some tests are better or fairer than others, but like it or not, the grades based on those tests are the measure of each student's success in school. Grades can determine whether students will be promoted or obtain a degree, get into an advanced program, and/or even find the job they want.

Because tests can have all these consequences, it is quite understandable that all students at one time or another will be anxious about tests. A certain amount of anxiety is normal—and even desirable—because it motivates students to try to do their best. Just as runners get themselves psyched up before a race, actors before a performance on stage, football players before a game, lawyers before a trial, and business executives before a meeting with important clients, so students need to get themselves psyched up before a big test.

Too much anxiety, however, can spoil a student's performance. If a student is too tense and too worried about doing well on a test, he or she will find it almost impossible to concentrate (Elliott, DiPerna, Mroch, & Lang, 2004). Check with your students to see if, when they try to read their class notes, the words seem like a meaningless blur. When they sit down to take the test, does their mind go blank? These are the signs of too much anxiety.

In this chapter, teachers will find out how to teach their students to prepare for a test without succumbing to panic. Students will learn how to psych themselves up for a test so they will be *motivated* to do their best; they will learn how to relax and how to organize the course content so they will be *able* to do their best. These are the first steps to becoming prepared.

PREPARING MENTALLY AND PHYSICALLY

Psyching Up

For students to do their best on a test, they need to be psyched up for it. Being psyched up helps one to focus all of one's attention on studying for and taking a test (Gettinger & Seibert, 2002). For most people, neither activity is fun, but when students realize that tests are the way we are evaluated in school and that they have to pass them to succeed, then students can psych up and go!

How do professional athletes and actors and executives psych themselves up? Studies of highly successful people have shown that their ability to keep their ultimate goals in mind is the key to their success (Andriessen, Phalet, & Lens, 2006; Cukras, 2006; Gabriele, 2007; Gettinger & Seibert, 2002; Goodstein, 1999; Klomegah, 2007).

Teachers can help students psych themselves up for a test by helping them visualize their ultimate goal and think about how the test is connected to it. Here are some questions for teachers to ask their students to help them make that connection. Try posing these questions to your students for their reflection when it is time for them to get ready for their next test.

1. What is my ultimate goal in life?

2. Why am I going to school?

3. What relationship does school have with my ultimate goal?

4. What relationship does this class have with my ultimate goal?

5. Is a good grade in this class important to my success in school?

6. Is a good grade in this class important to my being promoted or getting a degree?

7. Is a good grade in this class necessary to my qualifying for the advanced program of my choice?

8. Is a good grade in this class important to further my professional or career interests?

9. Is a good grade on this test important to my final grade in the class?

10. Will it be worthwhile to invest some time studying to get a good test grade?

11. Why is the information covered by this test important to learn?

12. How can the information learned for this test help me in my future pursuits?

13. Do I believe that if I set my mind to something, I can do it?

14. Do I have the ability to perform well on this test if I am prepared?

15. What do I have to do to get myself as *prepared* as possible for this test?

Relaxing

Once students are psyched up, they are ready to organize a game plan and get to work. But they need to know how to keep themselves from getting too much on edge. Teachers want their students to be psyched up to work but not so strung out that they get nothing accomplished. Remember, it is normal to feel anxious about tests, and anxiety can help students work harder and concentrate better—as long as they keep it under control. Prepared students are aiming for high productivity—*consistently* high. To do their best, they need to be highly motivated but not panicked.

In this section, students will discover that the best way to do this is to plan their schedules several days before a test so they will be able to get enough sleep, some physical exercise, and some quiet leisure time—and have enough time to study as well. Students will also learn some relaxation techniques and other ways to stay calm on the day of the test. Students who anticipate getting too anxious preparing for a test might want to review the material on relaxation.

Getting in Shape for a Test

Sleep is important. Staying up all night to study is usually not wise. It is more beneficial for students to get their normal eight (or six or ten) hours of sleep each night than to try to make up for an all-nighter by sleeping late the next day. Students need to be alert to study for a test as well as to take one. Regular sleep habits increase their chance of a good night's rest, and getting up at about the same time every morning means students won't have to rush to fit everything into the day's schedule.

It should be noted here, however, that once in a while, staying up all night to complete an important paper *is* acceptable. It can be an efficient use of a student's time where it means accomplishing an academic goal. The student will be judged on her performance, which in this case is the paper. Short of missing important class notes or sleeping through a test-preparation day, a student's degree of alertness following a term paper all-nighter is not so crucial. For a *test*, however, the performance takes place in school at the time of the test, and doing one's best requires being alert. This book does not advocate staying up all night for every paper, but if doing an occasional all-nighter is the only way to finish a paper and have prime hours available to study for a test, too, then that is the best use of time.

Apart from regular sleep habits, taking occasional breaks from studying for quiet leisure activities and for physical exercise also helps students to stay alert. Physical activities, such as running, working out, tennis, and handball, are good tension breakers as long as they are part of a normal routine. Students who do not normally engage in strenuous forms of exercise shouldn't start when they are studying for a test. Instead, a brisk walk or some moderate stretching will help relieve tension.

Students should allow some quiet relaxation time as well to reduce fatigue and tension (Brown & Schiraldi, 2004; Carlson, Hoffman, Gray, & Thompson, 2004). They can use meal times as breaks from studying and then spend a little more time in conversation, reading for pleasure, watching a movie or television show, or listening to music. Relaxing after a meal not only helps to reduce tension: It also improves digestion, which contributes to better health. Moreover, right after a meal, one is not as alert, so studying then will not be as effective as a half hour or an hour later.

A study break—whether involving physical activity or quiet relaxation—should be a reward for a student's hard work. The student should stop studying at the first sign of excessive fatigue. This does not mean the moment one feels a little tired but instead pushing oneself a little further by thinking of the reward, then stopping for a break when one has pushed oneself to the limit of one's concentration.

The teacher could ask students to write out a list of the kinds of relaxation breaks they find most appealing. Students could be encouraged to use them as rewards for studying hard.

But a break is only a break, and the teacher can likewise instruct the students that the activities they list must be used only for study *breaks,* not for *distractions* from studying. Anything that competes for their attention while they are preparing for a test should be avoided: radios, headsets, stereos, computers, television, the telephone, and other distractions should be reserved for *relaxation* breaks.

Staying Calm on Exam Day

When students know they are prepared—that they have followed their game plan to study for the test and know all the techniques for taking essay and objective tests—they will naturally feel more confident. But even prepared students can become unduly nervous just before and during a test. If this should happen, students should be able to fall back on some proven ways to offset nervousness before it gets too serious and they lose control.

Relaxation training is often helpful for students who experience frequent test panic. Some school counselors have training materials or programs (usually on cassettes or DVDs) that teach relaxation techniques. The basic concept of all these techniques is that relaxing physically makes it impossible for anyone to feel overly anxious. The training materials teach a person to relax at will, and with a bit of practice, a student can learn to relax while taking exams (Casbarro, 2004; Gates, 2005; Supon, 2004; Viadero, 2004).

Relaxation Techniques

There are a great many relaxation techniques. Here are a few easy ones for teachers to suggest to their students:

- Inhale deeply with your eyes closed, hold your breath, and then exhale slowly. Do this several times if you need to.
- Sit back in your chair and get as comfortable as possible. If your shoes feel uncomfortable, slip them off; no one will notice your feet under the desk or table.
- Try loosening up your entire body:
  - Tighten all your muscles from head to toe and hold them. Then let all your muscles loosen.
  - Tighten your muscles and then systematically (toes to feet to ankles to calves to knees and so on) loosen each part of your body.

The teacher should recommend that students practice these tension-breaking techniques before taking tests so they will be familiar with them at exam time. They can repeat them as often as necessary during the test. A number of other tricks can help students keep anxiety at a minimum just before and during a test:

1. *Get a good night's sleep.* Even though final cramming will be recommended later in the book as a test-preparation technique, it doesn't really call for staying up all night before a test!

2. *Eat some breakfast or lunch before the test,* but avoid greasy foods and foods with high acidity. Having food in the stomach may help calm nervousness and increase energy, but overeating could backfire, causing one to become sluggish and sleepy.

3. *Students should allow themselves the necessary time to get to their classrooms for a test.* If they are already nervous, rushing will only make them more so.

4. *Standing around and talking to others just before going in to take the test is not a good idea,* as it might only serve to confuse or unnerve the student. Instead, those precious moments before the test should be treated as an opportunity to quietly review condensed notes. (Techniques for condensing student notes will be explained in Chapter 3.)

5. A review of Chapter 6 will help students *be ready when they enter the testing room* and know just how to proceed.

6. Caution students *not to panic just because they are not writing busily while the others are.* Thinking and organizing are likelier to have a much bigger payoff than poorly thought out, hasty writing.

7. Similarly, *students should not be upset if other test takers finish sooner.* Prepared students will use as much time as is necessary to do well. Students who leave early may not be prepared and are not always the ones who get the best scores on a test ("Be a Better Test Taker!" 2002; Lester, 1991; Onwuegbuzie, 1994).

8. If it is impossible to avoid feeling very tense during the test, students should *remind themselves that they are players in this game.* Stress is part

of it; prepared students can hold up well under the stress. They will play the game and play it well; then they can leave and give themselves a deserved reward.

ORGANIZING YOUR COURSE CONTENT

All of the information in this chapter about getting in the proper frame of mind for tests and all the information in the rest of the book about studying for and taking tests will be of little use without a thorough knowledge and understanding of the content of the course that comes from class notes and reading. The rest of this chapter will suggest how to make class notes and do reading assignments in a way that will be useful to your students when it comes to test-study time.

Class Notes

When it comes time to study for a test, a thorough set of notes is essential. (Chapter 3 provides techniques for using notes to study for a test.) Great care in note taking from the very first day of class is crucial for later test-taking preparation (Barbarick & Ippolito, 2003; Cifuentes & Hsieh, 2003; Kobayashi, 2006; Kras, Strand, Abendroth-Smith, & Mathesius, 2002). Here are some tips for teachers to give to students to help them build an orderly and thorough set of notes. Students can start utilizing these tips in middle school and continue to hone note-taking skills throughout high school and into college.

1. *Go to all classes and take notes on everything the teacher emphasizes.* If possible, sit as close to the teacher as you can so you can hear and see everything.

2. *Be a good listener.* Be alert to what the teacher is saying as you take notes. Train yourself to concentrate on what is currently being said while recording ideas that have already been said.

3. *Keep notes for each class separate from notes for other classes.* This is easier if you use a loose-leaf binder or file folder rather than a spiral-bound notebook. You want to be able to reorganize your note pages and add handouts later when you study for tests.

4. *Take notes on the front side of the page only,* and record the name or number of the class and the date on each page.

5. *Use standard-sized notebook paper.* Try to leave spaces between topics as they change. (You'll find an example of class notes in Chapter 3, Figure 3.1.)

6. *Make your notes complete and clear enough so that they will have meaning later.* You should not write in full sentences; phrases are fine. Just be sure that they make sense to you and that you have captured the whole idea.

7. *If you missed something important, stay after class* and ask the teacher about it so you can fill in the gap in your notes.

8. *Write legibly.*

9. *Develop abbreviations* of common words and recurring terms so you can save time while taking lecture notes.

10. *Use a symbol,* such as an asterisk (*), to mark the points the teacher emphasizes.

11. *Keep assignments or suggestions for reading separate from class notes* but close enough to indicate which class they are related to. One good place is at the end of your notes on each topic.

12. *If ideas or examples come to mind as the teacher lectures, jot them down—* but label them "me" or identify them in some other way so you won't get your thoughts mixed in with the teacher's words.

13. *Be alert for clues to test items.* Sometimes the teacher will say, "This is important," or, "I might ask you this on a test," or, "You will see this again." You might want to asterisk and underline these items in your notes.

14. *Always record your teacher's examples exactly as they are given.* They might turn up again in a similar form on a test.

15. *Copy all charts, diagrams, and lists exactly as your teacher gives them.*

16. *Stay to the end of the class and keep taking notes to the end.* Sometimes teachers run out of time and crowd half the planned lecture into the last five minutes.

17. *Don't rely on a friend to take notes for you unless you* have *to be absent.* The notes may not be good, or even if they are, they may not trigger the same information for you as they do for someone else. Therefore, they will not be as effective as notes you take for yourself.

18. *If you are absent, copy someone's notes.* Try picking someone in class who takes good notes and knows what is going on. Read over the notes. If you do not understand something, ask the teacher first. If you can't ask the teacher, then ask the person who took the notes.

19. *At the end of the day, go over your notes from all of your classes.* Fill in the places that seem incomplete; in a week, your memory of the class won't be as clear. Wherever possible, it is an excellent idea to label your notes for each class by topics that were covered.

20. *Label any handouts with the course name or number and the date.* Later, group those handouts with the appropriate class notes by punching holes in the handouts and putting them behind the notes in your binder or folder.

Textbooks and Outside Reading

Students should keep up with their assigned textbook(s) and outside reading. There may come a time, however, when too much work comes all at once. This shouldn't be cause for panic (Barbarick & Ippolito, 2003; Gettinger & Seibert, 2002; Kras et al., 1999). Instead, students should complete as many of the steps listed below under "How to Read a Textbook Step-by-Step" as time allows. That way, they'll have at least some degree of familiarity with the material. To *survey quickly* the assigned textbook chapters or other reading and get an idea of the content, follow Steps 1 through 5. If there is time, skim the chapters to get a more detailed picture of their contents as directed in Step 6.

Step 7 tells how to *read* the assignment. Step 8 tells how to *take notes* on readings for test preparation after having read each chapter or section. Steps 7 and 8 will have to be omitted if students have a whole textbook to read in only a few days. The chapter notes collected in Step 8 can be valuable review material prior to chapter, unit, midterm, and final exams.

How to Read a Textbook Step-by-Step

Step 1: Pictures. Go through the entire chapter and look at all the pictures, tables, charts, diagrams, graphs, maps, and other illustrations. Read any written notations under or above the illustration for clarification, and read all the information in tables, charts, and other illustrations containing statistical data.

Step 2: Introduction. Most well-written chapters have an introduction. This will usually be the first few paragraphs. Read the introductory paragraphs to each assigned chapter and try asking yourself the factual questions that a reporter asks—*Who? What? Where? When?*—and the inferential questions that a reporter asks—*Why? How?*

Step 3: Bold Print. Read all the bold print from the beginning to the end of the chapter or section. Very often, the bold print serves as an outline of the chapter.

Step 4: Summary. Most well-written chapters have a summary or some type of wrap-up paragraphs. These will usually be at the very end of the chapter. Read the summary paragraphs.

Step 5: Questions. If there are questions or points for discussion in the chapter or at the end, read them over. These questions will often be clues about the most important information in the chapter.

Step 6: Skim. Starting at the beginning of the chapter, read the first and last sentence of each paragraph. The first sentence is usually a key one. The last sentence usually wraps up a thought and ties it in with the first sentence of the next paragraph. After reading the first sentence in a paragraph, skim through the following sentences until you come to the first word of the last sentence. Then read that sentence.

Step 7: Read. Starting at the beginning of the chapter, read it all the way through. Whenever you come to bold print, turn it into a question and read to answer that question.

Step 8: Note Taking. Fold a sheet of loose-leaf paper in half vertically. On the left half of the paper, write the boldfaced headings from the chapter. On the right half, write a few key words or phrases that will answer the questions you asked from the bold print in Step 7 as well as any words, phrases, or ideas that might show up as test items.

CHAPTER SUMMARY

It is normal for students to be nervous to a certain degree at test time. No matter how well prepared they are, they will still feel some tension. Teachers should instruct students not to be alarmed by this. Even the professional actor, lawyer, football player, runner, and business executive feel tense before a big event. These professionals let their tension work for them and help them sharpen their performance. Students can do the same: if they have prepared well for a test, which is their big event, the odds are very good they will do well because they are *prepared.*

Students know how to psych up when they can see the connection between their ultimate goals and the test. They know how to relax when they get too tense when they schedule their study time before a test to allow for leisure-time rewards and when they use relaxation techniques. And they know how to organize their course content by keeping thorough, systematic class notes and by reading their assignments for content, step by step.

2

How to Develop
a Game Plan

Time management is a basic survival skill in school. Time management means that students decide which tasks are most and least important, then schedule their time accordingly. This planning provides structure to their studying, frees them from uncertainty and guilt, and saves time by helping not to waste time (Gettinger & Seibert, 2002; Merrett & Merrett, 1997). Deciding how much time to spend studying for a test and what is most important to study is part of the game plan—an essential part of being prepared.

This chapter is filled with forms to help students figure out their study schedule and to help them decide what is most important to study in a limited amount of time. While filling out the forms may seem like extra work at first, after students have practiced using them, they will find that the forms save time and make studying more efficient. (An extra copy of each form is included in Appendix B at the back of the book for student practice.)

MASTER TEST SCHEDULE FOR THE TERM

The first step in preparing for a test is to develop a schedule of all the test dates for all the classes a student is taking in the given term. An especially important exam like a midterm or a final should be noted with the exam date and circled on each student's schedule(s). Students should be instructed to fill out their schedules in pencil, because their teachers might change dates or cancel tests and schedule new ones. Sometimes students do not have their exam schedules for an entire term, so they need to keep their master test schedules handy to keep them up-to-date.

Before students attempt to fill out the master test schedule for the term (Test Prep: Exercise 2.1), show your students the sample master test schedule for a fictitious student, Harry (Figure 2.1). Harry attends a school that uses the quarter system. Because there are only ten weeks in the school term, plus finals week, Harry has crossed out Weeks 11–16 on his master schedule.

Students can use Harry's test schedule to see if they can answer the planning questions in Test Prep: Exercise 2.1. (Answers to exercises can be found in Appendix A.)

TEST PREP: EXERCISE 2.1

1. What is the date of Harry's first test this term?

   _____

2. Which class is it for?

   _____

3. What is the content of that first test?

   _____

4. Is it a major test?

   _____

5. During Week 5, Harry has three tests. For which classes are they?

   _____

6. (a) His schedule indicates that two of the tests in Week 5 are on the same day. Which two are they?
   (b) Of the tests on the same day, for which one should Harry spend most of his time studying and why?

   _____

   _____

7. List the order of the tests that Harry should study for during Week 6.

   _____

8. During Weeks 2, 3, 4, 7, 8, and 9, Harry has two minor tests scheduled. One of the tests is always in _____. During any one of those weeks, does he have more than one test in one day?

   _____

   _____

9. Which test do you consider most important during Week 2? _____,
   during Week 3? _____, during Week 4? _____,
   during Week 7? _____, during Week 8? _____,
   during Week 9? _____. Why are these the most important weekly tests? _____

10. (a) List in order the tests that Harry should study for during finals week.

    _____

    _____

    (b) Which two finals will cover the most material?

    _____

    _____

    (c) Which finals will cover only material that came after the midterm test?

    _____

    _____

Figure 2.1

Harry's Master Test Schedule for Term

Test Dates & Content	Course Names					
	English	**Biology**	**Math**	**Psychology**		
Week 1	9/26 Vocab.					
Week 2	10/3 Vocab.		10/1 Ch. 1–3			
Week 3	10/10 Vocab.			10/7 Unit 1		
Week 4	10/17 Vocab.		10/15 Ch. 4–6			
Week 5	10/24 Vocab.		⟨10/24⟩ Midterm Ch. 1–6	10/21 Unit 2		
Week 6	⟨10/27⟩ Midterm Vocab. & Lit. (Ch. 1–9)	⟨10/31⟩ Midterm (Ch. 1–8)				
Week 7	11/7 Vocab.		11/5 Ch. 7–9			
Week 8	11/14 Vocab.			11/11 Unit 3		
Week 9	11/21 Vocab.		11/19 Ch. 10–12			
Week 10				11/25 Unit 4		
Week 11						
Week 12						
Week 13						
Week 14						
Week 15						
Week 16						
Finals Week	⟨12/10⟩ Vocab. & Lit. (Ch. 1–9)	⟨12/5⟩ Ch. 9–15	⟨12/8⟩ Ch. 7–12	⟨12/11⟩ Units 1–4		

After students have compared their answers to Test Prep: Exercise 2.1 with those in Appendix A, they should fill out their Master Test Schedule for Term. (An extra form is provided in Appendix B.) Students should be reminded to use pencil; include specific dates and content; and circle midterms, finals, and any other major tests.

PLANNING FOR EACH TEST

Now that students have an overview of their test schedules for the term, they should be encouraged to begin deciding how much and what to study for each test. Getting organized to study for a test is an essential part of being prepared (Gettinger & Seibert, 2002). This is the time for them to anticipate what may be on the test and decide what they will have to study. The first step students should take in getting organized is to answer the following questions (a form is provided for use with your students in Appendix B):

1. What do I already know about the topics?
2. What don't I know about the topics?
3. What clarifications do I need from my teacher?
4. What materials do I need to assemble to study?
5. What outside research do I need to do?
6. What reading do I still need to do?
7. What information seems most important?
8. How much time should I allow to prepare adequately for each area?
9. How much time do I actually have?
10. What is my game plan?

In the remainder of this chapter, material is presented that will help your students learn how to do a test analysis and use available files of old tests to answer Questions 1–7, learn how to make a study schedule for a test to make the answer to Question 9 come as close as possible to the answer to Question 8, and learn how to make a daily to-do list to prepare for a test. Together, the study schedule, the test analysis, and the list of things to do make up the "game plan." Their game plans are the answers to Question 10.

TEST ANALYSIS

It is very important that students know as much as possible about a test to plan their study schedule and preparation strategies. Teachers should encourage students to ask questions concerning a test and should schedule special review sessions before a major test. Teachers can encourage students to use a test analysis form during these sessions to predict the content and format of a test.

Even without a review session, however, students can obtain most of the information to complete a test analysis form through classes and reading. Students should fill out a test analysis form (photocopy the blank one in Appendix B or make your own) for each test during the term. Even though the form may at first seem to be a lot of extra trouble, it will be worth it when students get ready to study.

Students should be sure to fill in all the information they can get about a test on the form. Some of the blanks can be filled in from class notes and handouts. Often after taking the first test for a class, students will have more information about what to expect on future tests. For example, it is probable that the vocabulary tests that Harry will take in English during Weeks 2–5 and Weeks 7–9 will be a lot like the vocabulary test he took in Week 1. And the format for his psychology unit tests in Weeks 5, 8, and 10 is likely to resemble that of the Unit 1 test given in the third week of the term. Students should not assume they will all be exactly the same, however; they should ask their teachers.

Knowing the format of the test is highly valuable. Objective tests mean that students will have to be able to recognize answers, many of which will be specific facts. Subjective, or essay, tests mean that students will need an overall understanding of the content and be able to cite some specifics; they will have to generate the answers themselves rather than just recognize them. Knowing the total number of items on the test, the material to be covered, and the number of questions on each area of content will help them decide how to focus their studying and how to budget their study time. Comparing the number of questions to the time allowed will let them know if they will have to have quick recall or if they can take time to think. If they know who is writing and grading the test, they can anticipate particular biases—such as requiring correct spelling or preferring brief answers—and study accordingly.

What to Ask the Teacher

Teachers should encourage students to ask questions only about things they really need to know and that have not already been answered in class. Very often, if students listen attentively, a teacher will tell them a lot about an upcoming test as he lectures. Students cannot expect the teacher to give them the exact test questions, but often he or she will mention topics or chapters to study, specific areas of importance, or kinds of test questions to expect. A week or two before the test, the teacher might also be willing to answer specific questions from the test analysis form; however, students should also realize that the test might not be written that far in advance.

When students ask their teachers about tests, they should be tactful and should keep in mind that some questions on the form should not be asked of a teacher. For example, the question on biases is one for students to answer based on what they have observed in class or what students who have already taken the course have told them; it is not a question they should ask the teacher.

Utilizing Old Tests Made Available for Student Review

In addition to what students learn in class about an upcoming test, tests from previous terms can help them anticipate the content and format of their tests. Sometimes schools have a file of old tests that are available for student review. They can usually be found in the library, the counselors' offices, or in a reading and study skills center. Students can ask their teachers and their counselors if there are files of old tests that they might be allowed to use to help them prepare for an upcoming test. In addition, teachers may have copies of their own past class exams to share with interested students.

If students do review some old exams, they should use them to identify their general strengths and weaknesses. Copying and memorizing the questions on old exams will not help much. Instead, students should use them as guides to the type of test that might be given and the content that is likely to be emphasized.

In summary, students should use information from class and from past exams (if available) to fill in the test analysis form. They may not be able to fill in every blank, but the more information they have, the better they will be able to anticipate the test and the better they will be able to study for it.

A sample form for one of Harry's tests (Figure 2.2) gives an example of how a test analysis form can be filled out. Using this, students can answer the questions in Test Prep: Exercise 2.2 (comparing their answers with those at the back of the book in Appendix A). After they have studied this sample form, students will be ready to fill out their own test analysis form for an upcoming test (another blank form is included in Appendix B).

STUDY SCHEDULES FOR EACH TEST

A study schedule will ensure that students will have time to prepare thoroughly and efficiently for a test. The schedule will help them decide priorities for study and make commitments to themselves. When planning a schedule for test preparation, students will need to decide when to start studying and how much to study. To help students make these decisions, ask them the following questions (a form is provided in Appendix B for students to use):

1. How much time is available to study for this test?

2. Where do I stand now in the class, and how important is the test? How good of a grade do I need on this test?

3. How much time does the test analysis form indicate that I will need to study adequately for the test?

Figure 2.2

Test Analysis Form

Class	Psychology	**Teacher**	Parker
Date of Test	10/7	**Time of Day**	1:15
% of Grade	12.5%	**Major or Minor Test**	Minor

What is the format of the test?

Essay:	✓	Long-Answer (discuss, trace, compare and contrast)
	✓	Short-Answer (list, name, define, identify)
Objective:		True/False
		Multiple Choice
		Matching
		Completion (fill-in-the-blank)

How many questions will be on the test? ___4___

How many of each kind of question will be on it?

_2_ Long-Answer Essay		_____ True/False
_2_ Short-Answer Essay		_____ Multiple-Choice
		_____ Matching
		_____ Completion

How much time will I have for the test? ___1 hour___

What is the *content* of the test? ___Unit 1___

Topics or Kinds of Problems	Sources of Content (notes, readings, labs)	Format of Questions*	% of Score and # of Questions
What is psychology & how is it diff. from psychiatry?	Text: Ch. 1 plus class notes	Long-Answer Essay: discuss and contrast	30%/1
History of psych. and four schools of psych.	Text: Ch. 2 plus class notes	Long-Answer Essay: trace and discuss	30%/1
Major fields of psych.	Text: Ch. 3 plus class notes	Short-Answer Essay: identify and define	20%/1
Methods of psych.	Text: Ch. 4 plus class notes	Short-Answer Essay: lift and define	20%/1

(Continued)

Figure 2.2 (Continued)

Are details or general concepts important? _Both_

Do I have to know formulas or theorems? _No_ If so, which ones?*

Do I have to know definitions? _Yes_ If so, which ones?* _the major fields of psychology, the methods of psychology_

Do I have to know important names and dates? _Yes_ If so, which ones?* _for history of psych (time periods but not specific dates); Plato, Aristotle (early days); Hobbes, Locke (1600s); Wilhelm, Wundt (1879) —structuralism; Watson, Pavlov (1913) —behaviorism; Wertheimer, Hobbes, Koffka, Lewin (early 1900s) —Gestalt; Freud (early 1900s) —psychoanalysis_

Will points be taken off for spelling errors? _No, as long as word can be recognized_

Can I bring a dictionary to use during the test? _No_

Can I bring a calculator to use during the test? _Not Applicable (NA)_

If problems have to be worked out, how much credit is given for accuracy? _NA_,

and how much credit is given for method? _NA_

Will this be an open-book test? _No_

Are copies of previous exams available for inspection? _No_

Is this a departmental test or one made up by the teacher? _Teacher_

Who will grade this test?** _Teacher_

Do the writer and grader of this test have any special biases?**

Additional Clues or Notes:**

Be sure to emphasize everything we emphasized in class when I answer questions.

Notes:
* You may not be able to find this out before the test.
** You shouldn't ask this question of the teacher.

TEST PREP: EXERCISE 2.2

1. The material that Harry will have to study comes from two sources. What are they?

    _____

2. To prepare for this test, should Harry refer to the sections in this book on objective tests?

    _____

3. (a) Which are the two most important areas of content for this test?

    _____

    _____

    (b) How do you know?

    _____

    _____

    (c) Which kinds of questions will be asked on these two most important areas?

    _____

    (d) Should Harry spend more time studying these two areas than the others? Why?

    _____

    _____

    _____

4. (a) Will Harry have to do much memorizing for this test?

    _____

    (b) What are some of the things he will have to memorize?

    _____

    _____

    _____

5. When studying for the test, should Harry concentrate on his class notes?

    _____

How Much Time Is Available?

To develop a study schedule for a test, students first need to see how much time is not already committed in the two weeks before the test. After they have crossed out the hours when they will be going to class, working, doing out-of-class assignments and papers, and sleeping, the hours left are those available for studying for a test.

To see what a study schedule looks like, turn to Figures 2.3 and 2.4. These are Harry's study schedules for the week before and the week of his psychology exam. Note that the only activities with a label are his tests; for all other activities, the hours have simply been crossed out. The blank hours are those available for studying for the tests.

Looking at Harry's schedules, we can see that during the week of his psychology test he also has a test in English, but it is three days after his psychology test. Because the vocabulary test is a minor one and he has study time available for it after his psychology test, he doesn't need to worry about studying for it until after the psychology test. The week before the psychology exam, Harry has a math test on Wednesday and a vocabulary test on Friday. It looks as though he will need to use his test-study time that week (through Friday) getting ready for those two tests. Thus, the times that Harry has available to study for the psychology exam are Saturday and Sunday, Monday afternoon and evening, and Tuesday morning.

In Appendix B are blank schedules for the week before and the week of an exam. Students can cross out the hours for fixed activities—including paper writing and sleeping—to see how much time is left to study for the next major exam. They should also be sure to write in all the other tests they will have to take during those two weeks. (Another set of schedules is included in Appendix B for use with students.)

Determining Test Value

Now that students have counted the hours they have available to study for the next major test, they need to consider where they stand in that class, how much the test counts, and how important a good grade on the test will be. Teachers should help students to figure out their course average before the test and then refer to their test analysis form to see how much the test counts toward their final grade in the course. Generally, the lower a student's course average and the more important the test, the more important it is to try for a high grade and to spend more hours studying. On the other hand, the higher the course average and the less important the test, the less important it is to use all available hours to study for it.

How Much Time Does a Student Need to Study Adequately?

Students should look at their test analysis form to see what will be covered on the test. Next, students should assess where they are currently in terms of reading, other assignments, labs, and problems that must be

Figure 2.3

Schedule

Week Before ___*Psychology*___ **Test**

AM

	Mon.	Tues.	Wed.	Thurs.	Fri.	Sat.	Sun.
12–1							
1–2							
2–3							
3–4							
4–5							
5–6							
6–7							
7–8							
8–9							
9–10					Vocab. Test		
10–11							
11–12			Math Test				

PM

	Mon.	Tues.	Wed.	Thurs.	Fri.	Sat.	Sun.
12–1							
1–2							
2–3							
3–4							
4–5							
5–6							
6–7							
7–8							
8–9							
9–10							
10–11							
11–12							

Figure 2.4

Schedule

Week of _Psychology_ **Test**

AM

	Mon.	Tues.	Wed.	Thurs.	Fri.	Sat.	Sun.
12–1							
1–2							
2–3							
3–4							
4–5							
5–6							
6–7							
7–8							
8–9							
9–10					Vocab. Test		
10–11							
11–12							

PM

	Mon.	Tues.	Wed.	Thurs.	Fri.	Sat.	Sun.
12–1							
1–2		Psych. Test					
2–3							
3–4							
4–5							
5–6							
6–7							
7–8							
8–9							
9–10							
10–11							
11–12							

completed in preparation for the particular test. Here are seven steps that teachers can use to help their students make that assessment:

1. List the required readings that will be covered by the test.

2. Check off those that you have done.

3. List any other required assignments, labs, or problems on which the test may be based.

4. Check off those that you have done.

5. Look at what still needs to be done before you can begin to study.

6. Try to determine how much of the test will be based on work you still need to do.

7. Figure out how much time it will take you to do that work.

If students have a lot of work still to complete but not enough available study hours to finish it as well as study for the test properly, they will need to find ways to cut corners to complete the reading and other assignments. For example, they can use Steps 1–5 from Chapter 1 (page 14) to survey the reading quickly and get an overall idea of its content. Or they can skim the problems left to do, and if more than one uses a particular concept or theorem, work only one. Based on how much of the test will come from these incomplete assignments, students should decide how much time they will spend on each of them.

Through this decision-making process, students will be setting priorities; some parts of the content need more time alloted than others. Students will need some flexibility in their study schedule, too, should a particular reading, assignment, or problem turn out to be more difficult than anticipated. Nor should students forget to allow some time for social activities and study breaks. In short, they should be reasonable in planning their study schedule; a study plan that demands every minute of every available hour will be impossible to live up to. Being a prepared student is not easy; it involves not only commitment and persistence, but also good judgment—that is, knowing which material to focus on and which to review lightly or to even ignore.

PLANNING TEST-STUDY TIME

When Harry looks at the test analysis form for his psychology test (Figure 2.2), he sees that he has done only half the required reading for the test and still has to read Chapters 3 and 4 in his textbook. Each chapter and his class notes on them will make up 20 percent of the test, so they are important. Although this is not a major test, accounting for only 12.5 percent of his final grade in the course, Harry decides that trying to do well is important because it is the first test in the class. He knows that first impressions count and wants the teacher to consider him a good student.

Looking at his schedules for the week before and the week of the test (Figures 2.3 and 2.4), he notes that the open times on Saturday, Sunday, Monday, and Tuesday before the test are the only hours he has to prepare. Harry decides to use the study time available on Saturday to read Chapters 3 and 4 and take notes to answer test questions from those chapters. He will also go through his class notes on those chapters so he can fill in gaps with text notes. He plans to use the available time on Sunday to go back to Chapters 1 and 2 and take notes to help answer the test questions on those Chapters. He will also look over the class notes he has on those chapters. (In Chapters 3–5 of this book, the techniques for studying reading and class notes are presented with exercises for you to use with students.)

Studies of students preparing for tests have shown that the most important study time is the day and night before the test (A. L. Raygor, personal communication, 1982). Although long-range preparation and keeping up with class work is also very important, reviewing and reciting material the day and night before an exam is beneficial (Flippo, Becker, & Wark, in press). Harry is saving this most important time for reviewing and reciting. On Monday, he will study for the test by going back over all his notes and then writing answers to the questions he anticipates will be on the test. On Tuesday morning, he will review again so that all the information will be fresh in his mind when he walks in to take the test at 1:15 PM that day.

Figure 2.5 shows Harry's list of the things he needs to study for his psychology test, including when he plans to study them. Teachers can read over Harry's list with their students and then help students make one for their own study time before their next test. Students can use the test analysis form and the schedules they filled out. (Another things-to-do list can be found in Appendix B.)

To make sure that he will complete each day's allotment of things to do, Harry breaks down his game plan for test study into daily lists of things to do and writes each day's list on an index card to carry with him wherever he goes during the day. Before going to bed the night before a day of test preparation, Harry will make a list of the things that have to be accomplished the next day and number them in the order they need to be done. The next day, he will cross off each item after he completes it. If he does not finish everything on the card, he can put the tasks left to do at the top of the next day's card. Writing each day's tasks on a card is a motivational device; it not only forces Harry to specify study time, but it also causes him to make a commitment to himself to complete each study task. If he does not finish everything on the list, he is likely to feel guilty.

Teachers can show students Harry's daily list for Saturday, his first day of test preparation (Figure 2.6), and then help students make their own daily lists on index cards based on their things-to-do lists. Students can use the box on page 147 for their first card.

Figure 2.5

Harry's Things-to-Do List

**Things to Do
to Study for** _Psychology_ **Test**   **Day or Date** _Tues._   **Time** _1:15 PM_

Task	Day	Time
Read Ch. 3 in text	Sat.	9:00–10:30 AM
Read Ch. 4 in text	Sat.	2:00–3:30 PM
Take notes on Chs. 1–4 to answer test questions:		
Ch. 1	Sun.	900–10:00 AM
Ch. 2	Sun.	Noon–1:00 PM
Ch. 3	Sat.	11:00 AM–Noon
Ch. 4	Sat.	4:00–5:00 PM
Go back over notes on all chapters (class & text) to answer test questions:		
Ch. 1	Sun.	10:30–11:30 AM
Ch. 2	Sun.	1:30–2:30 PM
Ch. 3	Sat.	12:30–1:30 PM
Ch. 4	Sat.	5:30–7:00 PM
Write an answer to each test question for the following:		
Ch. 1	Mon.	1:00–2:00 PM
Ch. 2	Mon.	2:15–3:15 PM
Ch. 3	Mon.	3:30–4:30 PM
Ch. 4	Mon.	4:45–5:45 PM
Take notes on each of the answers.	Mon.	7:00–9:00 PM
Memorize notes on each of the answers.	Tues.	8:00–10:00 AM
Read over answers one more time.	Tues.	10:00–11:00 AM
Recite and cram from notes.	Tues.	11:00 AM–Noon
Leave for school.	Tues.	Noon
Arrive at school.	Tues.	12:45 PM
Recite and cram from notes.	Tues.	12:45–1:15 PM

Figure 2.6

Harry's Daily List

Saturday
1. Look at test questions for Ch. 3.
2. Read Ch. 3 to answer questions.
Take notes to answer question.
3. Go back over class notes to answer Ch. 3 questions.
4. Group chap. notes and class notes on Ch. 3.
5. Look at test questions for Ch. 4.
6. Read Ch. 4 and take notes to answer questions.
7. Go back over class notes to answer Ch. 4 questions.
8. Group chap. notes and class notes on Ch. 4.

Planning for Midterms and Finals

To prepare for major tests, students should generally follow the planning and scheduling procedures already described in this chapter. There are a couple of differences, however. Because there are usually many major tests within days of each other, students should allow two to three, rather than one to two, weeks to study. Also, students will have to establish more detailed priorities for what they need to accomplish. (Note: A planning form for two weeks before a test is included in Appendix B.)

Because students are under pressure to work especially hard for midterms and finals, they will need to use special decision-making strategies to get through them with the best grades possible. Here are some tips for teachers to give to students to use during the two to three weeks before midterms and finals.

1. Follow all the organizing, evaluation, and planning strategies described in this book.

2. Figure out what your present grade is in each class.

3. Look at your test analysis forms and all available past exams for each major test and estimate how much time will be needed to prepare for each of them. Which tests will require more effort and which ones less?

4. Figure out how much catch-up work needs to be done for each class. Plan to do catch-up work early and only on content you think will be on the exams.

5. Rank these big tests in order of importance.

6. Use that ranking to set priorities for catching up and studying for your exams.

7. Starting two to three weeks before the tests, catch up with the reading and other course work according to your priorities.

8. Two weeks before the tests, begin studying your class notes, readings, and other assignments.

9. Follow the procedures for studying for the specific kinds of exams described in Chapters 3–5 of this book.

10. Follow the procedures for taking the specific kinds of exams described in Chapters 6–8 of this book.

GAME PLAN CHECKLIST

To make sure students' game plans for studying for each test are complete, teachers can ask students to check off the items on the following list as they get them done. (A game plan checklist designed for students' future use is included in Appendix B.)

_____ 1. Did I prepare a *master test schedule* for the term, putting in all the dates?

_____ 2. Did I cross out all my fixed commitments on the schedules *for one week before the test and the week of the test* (two weeks before midterm and final tests) and note when I have other tests during those weeks?

_____ 3. Did I figure out when I have *study time available* on these schedules for each test?

_____ 4. Did I prepare a *test analysis form* using information from class, from the teacher, and from other sources?

_____ 5. Have I checked to see if *past exams* are available for review?

_____ 6. Using my test analysis form and past exams (if they were available to me), did I determine the *format of the test* so I know whether to prepare for objective or essay questions?

_____ 7. Using my test analysis form, did I assess *where I am right now* in terms of reading and other assignments related to the test?

_____ 8. Did I make a complete *list of things to do* to prepare for the test, putting the most important items first and planning when to do them according to the time available on my study schedule?

_____ 9. Do I realize that I need to break down the things-to-do list into *daily lists* and put these on cards for an each-day reminder?

Once students have completed and checked off all the items on the game plan checklist, they are ready for the next step—preparing and studying for the test!

CHAPTER SUMMARY

Preparing students involves helping your students know the importance of getting organized to take a test.

Students should not just plunge in haphazardly and hope for the best. *Prepared students* have a game plan for their study, which means that they do the following:

- Very carefully think things through and organize for the test.
- Break tasks down into smaller ones.
- Decide the order in which the tasks will be done.
- Set time limits for the completion of each task.
- Attend to one thing at a time.
- Build in relaxation rewards along the way.
- Learn relaxation-training techniques in preparation for exam time.

PART TWO

Preparing for All Tests

3

Strategies for Test Study

For most of the tests your students take, they are not allowed to refer to their notes or their textbooks. So to do well, they must be able to recall the important information from memory. In this chapter, they will learn how to organize their resources (class notes, reading, and other assignments) so they can make study notes to use for memorizing key facts and concepts. Students will also learn a number of ways to memorize as well as the importance of cramming (which is really last-minute memorizing and reviewing) just before a test. All these are techniques students can use to study for every kind of objective and essay test.

MEMORIZING

Teachers can explain to their students that one's memory is like a computer. It stores information for later retrieval. Good memory is developed. Material has to be read and reviewed, classified and organized, reviewed and condensed, and reviewed some more.

To prepare better for tests, students should be taught that there are three faculties to the memory process: retention, recognition, and recall. Retention is the capacity for remembering. Recall means retrieving stored information from your memory bank. To recall information, you must depend on your memory alone, while to recognize information, you are given an aid or a cue. Thus, recognition is easier than recall. A multiple-choice test uses recognition; you recognize the right answers because you've seen them before. An essay test requires recall. Research indicates that students who prepare for essay exams usually do better than those who prepare for objective exams, even if the exam is objective. This is probably because when students study for an essay exam, they learn a lot of information and practice recalling it, but when studying for an objective exam, they learn only enough to recognize the correct answers. So the prepared student studies thoroughly—to know the material well enough to recall it—even for an objective test.

Thoroughly knowing the material means committing it to long-term rather than short-term memory. Short-term memory is fleeting and limited. An example of short-term memory is when you dial information to get a telephone number, mentally or verbally repeat the number, dial the number, and then forget it. The number was never internalized and stored. When new information is added to short-term memory, old information is pushed out.

Long-term memory internalizes and stores information within the mind for later use. Information that is particularly appealing and important goes into long-term memory. That information is often used and repeated and becomes part of the memory bank.

Most of the material that students have to learn for tests is neither appealing nor important enough to become part of long-term memory easily. Instead, it usually falls into the same category as the phone number that was needed only once. Without repetition or concentrated reviewing and reciting, most material studied for a test will be pushed out of one's memory rapidly. Consequently, repetition and reciting must be a part of a student's exam study procedure. One cannot store all of the material in one's long-term memory, but through increased familiarity, the student will be able to retain most of it and recall it during an exam.

Research indicates that overlearning and thoroughly mastering material improves recall of it (Gettinger & Seibert, 2002). This means that students should go through the hard work of analyzing, categorizing, note taking, predicting, practicing, and condensing all the material to be learned. Because research also shows that new learning can displace what was previously studied, they should review and recite just before the exam. This ensures that the material will be most accessible when it is needed.

ORGANIZING RESOURCES

Students should be instructed that the first step in memorizing the necessary information for their tests is to collect all the textbooks, notes, library materials, and other resources that might contain exam material. Students should go through the information on their test analysis forms carefully and be sure they have all the resources together in the location where they will study. They need a quiet and private spot where they can spread out their materials and know they will be left undisturbed.

Once their materials are all together, students should begin to organize them (Cifuentes & Hsieh, 2003). They should mark important pages in their text and other books with paper-clipped notes indicating the topics. Then they should go back and make a list of the pages they will need to review. They should next pull out all their pertinent class notes and try to group them either by each of the anticipated exam topics or by the topics covered in their class notes.

TEST PREP: EXERCISE 3.1

Figure 3.1 shows Harry's notes from his psychology class. Have students organize them according to the following topics, which are based on his test analysis form:

1. What is psychology, and how is it different from psychiatry?
2. Relate the history of psychology and describe the four schools of psychology.
3. Describe the major fields of psychology.
4. Describe the methods of psychology.

Tell students that if they think certain notes should be categorized under the topic "What is psychology, and how is it different from psychiatry?" they should write a *1* next to the notes. If they think certain notes should be categorized under the topic "Relate the history of psychology and describe the four schools of psychology," they should write a *2* next to those notes, and so on. If they think certain notes do not fit any of the categories Harry expects to be on his test, they should write *NA* (not applicable) next to those notes; these need not be included with the notes to review and study. (The answers for Exercise 3.1 are in Appendix A.)

Figure 3.1

Harry's Psychology Class Notes

Abnormal Psych. — studies all forms of abnormal human behavior.
Clinical Psych. — deals with normal and abnormal behavior and with indiv. psychol.
adjustment to oneself and one's environment.
Comparative Psych. — studies behavior and abilities of different animal species.
Developmental Psych. — studies changes in human behavior from birth to old age.
Educational Psych. — applies the principles of psych. to the ed. process.
Psychology is the science that studies why human beings and animals behave as they do.
The psychologist is interested in understanding the whole range of human experience.
Psychology is one of the behavioral sciences, like biology, sociology, and anthropology.
Psychiatry is a medical science dealing with mental illness. Psychology studies all kinds
of behavior, normal as well as abnormal. Psychiatrists are physicians with MD degrees
and special training in the field of mental illness. Most psychologists have PhD or
MA degrees instead of medical school training.

(Continued)

Figure 3.1 (Continued)

1. Experiments — the experimental method enables a psychologist to control the conditions that determine the aspect of behavior being studied.
2. Natural observation — the direct observation of human behavior in its natural environment.
3. Case histories — collection of info. about an individual's past and present life.
4. Surveys — the psychol. interviews members of a group by means of written questionnaires or orally. The psychol. can pull the info. together and draw conclusions about average attitudes or behavior.

Psychological problems are often categorized by the terms (1) neurosis, (2) psychosis, (3) paranoia, (4) schizophrenia, and (5) depression.

Behaviorism — Watson's (1913) reaction against structuralism. Watson called for the study of the observable behavior of humans and animals — not of their experiences.

Gestalt psychology — concerned with the organization of mental processes — we perceive organized patterns and the whole — Wertheimer, Kohler, Koffka, Lewin.

Psychoanalysis — Freud (early 1900s) developed a theory to explain why people become emotionally disturbed — people repress the needs and desires that are unacceptable to themselves or society.

Careers in psychology — for info., write Amer. Psych. Assoc., 1200 17th St. NW, Washington, DC 20036

Industrial psych. — applies psych. principles and techniques to the needs and problems of industry.

Physiological psych. — concerned with relationship between behavior and the function of the nervous system.

Social psych. — studies relationships among people in groups and the formation of public opinion.

Personality studies — studies the diff. characteristics of people and how these characteristics develop and can be measured.

Perception studies — studies the process by which patterns of environmental energies become known as objects, events, people, and other aspects of the world.

Structuralism — Wundt — thought main purpose of psych. was to describe and analyze conscious experience, including sensations, images, and feelings of which only the person himself is aware.

MAKING STUDY NOTES

Once students have organized all their material by exam topic, they should read it through and take notes. As they take these notes, they will be reviewing and learning the material. Then they can use the notes to memorize the material. To facilitate memorization, students should cluster the facts and ideas into meaningful categories. Teachers can tell students that there are several ways to do this, depending on which is most appropriate for the material they need to memorize: by topic on index cards, in lists in a steno pad, or in outlines or diagrams on notebook paper.

Topic Cards

You can point out to your students that this method works especially well for foreign language and other vocabulary study. It is also excellent for natural and biological science material, where there are classification systems to learn. Each card should be labeled by exam topic. In this way, students will be able to add or delete cards as needed; as they learn the material on a card, they can set it aside. They will also be able to rearrange the cards as needed while studying.

Lists

Another good method of making study notes you can share with your students, especially when reviewing factual material, is lists. In a stenographer's notebook, students should write the general topic and subtopic in the left-hand column and, in the right-hand column, make a list of all relevant concepts and facts they come across as they view their reading and class notes.

The example in Figure 3.2 shows Harry's notes on psychoanalysis in list format on a stenographer's notebook.

Figure 3.2

Notes in a List

Schools of psychology:	
Psychoanalysis	early 1900s
	Freud
	developed theory to explain why people
	become emotionally disturbed
	people repress needs/desires that are
	unacceptable to themselves or society

Outlines

Tell your students that this method of making notes works best when relationships among sets of information are important. It can also help them gain a perspective on the relation of each component to the whole. When using an outline, they should list each topic as the major heading. Next they should divide the topic into its major subtopics, with each major subtopic as a separate heading and further divided into its parts. Under each of these parts, they will list the pertinent details and supportive information.

The example in Figure 3.3 shows Harry's psychology notes on the difference between psychology and psychiatry in outline format.

Figure 3.3

Notes in an Outline

Differences Between Psychology and Psychiatry

I. Psychology
   A. Behavioral Science
      1. Studies why human beings and animals behave as they do.
      2. Studies the whole range of human experience.
         (a) Normal
         (b) Abnormal
   B. Psychologists usually have PhD or MA degree.

II. Psychiatry
   A. Medical Science
      1. Deals with abnormal behavior of human beings.
      2. Deals mostly with mental illness.
   B. Psychiatrists are physicians with MDs and special training in mental illness.

Diagrams

When we use the family tree, or diagram, method of taking notes, we are laying out the material in diagrammatic form. Have the students put the topic or central idea in a box at the top of the page and then link subtopics or subsections of associated information in boxes joined by straight lines. The location of these boxes and the lines connecting them will be determined by the relationships among the various components of information being noted.

Figure 3.4 uses Harry's psychology notes on Gestalt psychology to illustrate the diagram technique.

CONDENSING STUDY NOTES

To memorize one's study notes, it is helpful to condense them. The thinking and writing students do to condense their already categorized notes is

Figure 3.4

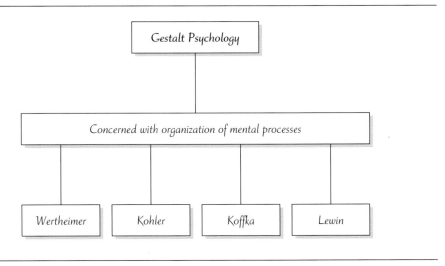

in fact part of the memorization process. A student's primary objective, however, should be to reduce his or her stack of notes for each topic into a smaller amount covering the important specifics of each topic. Having reduced the notes once, the student should attempt to condense them even further—in effect, condensing the condensed notes. With each reduction, the student absorbs more into memory as well as getting a more workable set of notes for later review.

When condensing their study notes, students can use whatever system seems to work best for them—topic cards, lists, outlines, or diagrams. It is best to write condensed notes on index cards, which are durable and easy to handle when memorizing and reciting. Students can conveniently carry these with them to study during idle moments. Index cards can also be sorted easily and can be set aside when students are finished with any part of them.

Students should write their condensed notes on only one side of each card and remember to keep the notes categorized all through the condensing process. As to how to know when to stop condensing their notes, a good rule of thumb is to condense them until they just about stop making sense.

Once their notes are condensed to the limit, students are ready to begin formal memorization. Here are some pointers they can use to memorize the information they have condensed in their notes:

1. *Memorize and recite small groups of material.* Organize your cards into small groups by topic. Memorize your categorized cards one small group at a time. Recite what you've memorized, then set the cards aside. Go on to another small group of cards. Later, come back to the first group of memorized cards and review and recite again.

2. *Memorize what you don't know but keep reviewing what you do know.* Spend most of the time studying the cards you aren't sure of. But periodically review and recite learned cards.

3. *Change the order of topics learned.* After you have been through all the topics at least once, shuffle the cards within each topic area and study them again. If you are relying on the order of the topics as a memory cue, you may have trouble on the test, which will probably not use the same order.

MEMORIZATION TECHNIQUES

To memorize the information in condensed study notes, a variety of techniques can be employed. Students should experiment with them and use the ones that are most appropriate to the kind of information they want to memorize. A few examples follow.

Memory Search and Association

To memorize a specific piece of information, search your memory for anything in your past experience or knowledge that relates to it. If you can recall any related information, you probably can remember the new information by connecting it to what you already know. For example, to remember the difference between the terms *inflation* and *depression* for an economics test, you might remember that inflating a tire makes it get bigger (with inflation, prices get bigger, or higher), while depression means feeling down (with depression, all economic activity slows down).

Mnemonic Connection

Aid your memory by some artificial device or connection. Does a term sound or look like any word you already know? If so, make up an imaginary connection between the two. Does the first syllable of the new term match the first syllable of any words you know that could be used as a connection? Does the first letter of each word in a list or a group of words form an acronym, or a group of letters that you'll remember, to trigger your recall of the list? For example, to remember the title *American Federation of Labor and Congress of Industrial Organizations*, we use the acronym AFL-CIO. If you need to remember the names of the Big Four allied countries during World War II, you could use the acronym GRUC (Great Britain, Russia, the United States, and China).

Often, a catchy phrase will help you remember the order of something difficult to memorize. For example, for a music test, to recall the names and order of the notes on the lines of the treble clef staff, you could remember the phrase *Every Good Boy Does Fine* (E, G, B, D, F). For an astronomy test, to recall the order of the planets and other celestial bodies, and their proximity to the sun, remember the phrase *My Very Eager Mother Just Served Us Nine Pizzas* (My = Mercury; Very = Venus; Eager = Earth; Mother = Mars; Just = Jupiter; Served = Saturn; Us = Uranus; Nine = Neptune; Pizzas = Pluto).

Whole Learning

When there is a large, integrated body of facts and concepts, look over the material from beginning to end to see how it is related. Let your headings form the core of your study. Think of how the material is interrelated. Look for principles, ideas, and concepts running through the material.

If you are memorizing a short poem, prose, a speech, theorem, or formula, repeat the whole thing over and over until it is memorized. If you are memorizing a long selection, divide it into two or three logical units. When they are learned, put them together and practice reciting the whole selection.

Recite and Write

To promote recall, it is important to use some kind of physical activity. Say aloud or write in your own words the ideas and facts you want to remember. Writing or reciting helps you transfer into your memory bank what might have been a fleeting piece of information. The amount of reciting or writing depends on the material. If you need to memorize lists of names, dates, or formulas, reciting or writing can take a considerable amount of time. If you need to memorize ideas, theories, or comparisons, reciting or writing will not be as time consuming.

Cramming

The term *cramming* has acquired a bad connotation because it is often used to describe students who didn't take time to prepare for an exam earlier and so must stay up most of the night before, trying to do all the necessary studying. But the term can also mean studying for an exam for several days and reviewing, reciting, and memorizing condensed notes just before going to bed—for a good night's sleep—the night before the exam.

You should let your students know that final cramming can be an essential and desirable aspect of exam preparation. As already stressed, repetition, reviewing, and reciting are essential for memorization. Forgetting happens very rapidly; therefore, a student really must repeat, review, recite, and review again almost up to the last minute so that the memorized material will not become displaced or lost.

Whether we call studying "memorizing" or "cramming" depends on when it takes place. Memorizing is the rote repetition, review, and reciting we do whenever we try to learn something we need to retain. Final cramming is the rote repetition, review, and reciting we do just before an exam to keep information fresh in our minds.

Research has shown that forgetting takes place faster when we are awake and more slowly while we are sleeping (Bower, 2007; Kim, 2005; A. L. Raygor, personal communication, 1982; Stickgold, Hobson, Fosse, & Fosse, 2001). If material is crammed just before going to sleep, it will be remembered longer than material learned before other activities. So it would be a big mistake for a student who had spent several days preparing for an exam to listen to friends who suggested a movie the night before, saying, "You deserve a break!" or "It's too late to study now." The night before the exam is a good time to study. So the student should do final cramming and then go right to bed and get a good night's sleep. The next morning, as a follow-up, find time to final cram some more and read over answers to the predicted test questions right up to exam time.

CHAPTER SUMMARY

To study for any kind of test, students need to start several days in advance, collecting and organizing all their materials—class notes, textbooks, outside reading, and class assignments. They should make study notes on the material, topic by topic; condense those notes as tightly as they can and memorize them; and review and recite the information until they know it thoroughly. Cramming the night before the exam is a good idea, but they should get a good night's sleep, too. They can cram some more the next morning before leaving to take the test—then review, recite, and cram right up to exam time. The worst thing they can do is give themselves the opportunity to begin forgetting!

4

Preparing for Essay Questions and Tests

Teachers give essay questions and tests because they want to make an in-depth assessment of students' knowledge of the course content. An essay exam measures higher levels of the student's understanding of content than an objective exam. By using good essay questions, the teacher can tell how well a student can analyze, evaluate, and apply the concepts and information presented in the course.

Students need to be able to predict the questions on the test and practice writing essay answers to them. To predict the questions, they can use the test analysis form from Chapter 2 (Figure 2.2). To practice the answers, they can use their organized study notes, which they learned how to make in Chapter 3. The questions they predict will help them decide what information to memorize and review. Teaching students the information contained in this chapter and having them work through the exercises will give them some experience in predicting short- and long-answer essay questions and in practicing how to answer them.

PREDICTING QUESTIONS

The easiest way for students to predict questions is for the teacher to tell them what will be on the test. Alternatively, you can have them turn to their test analysis form as well as their class notes and reading assignments and make a list of the emphasized topics. Then they can begin developing the topics into essay questions. Even if their predicted questions don't turn out to be exactly like those on the exam, by developing their own questions, they will have been actively thinking about and learning the material.

It sometimes helps if they work on predicting questions with a partner taking the same course. They can each go through their own notes and predict questions, each one perhaps picking up some important notes or areas of emphasis the other missed. Often, it is possible to reach a greater understanding about a concept or theory by discussing one's notes with a partner and predicting questions together. A word of caution, however: as many students have problems with concentration when studying with others, they should limit joint study to predicting questions together.

Different kinds of essay questions require somewhat different kinds of answers. This chapter presents some ideas for teaching students how to fit the various kinds of questions to the kinds of information they will encounter in a course.

SHORT-ANSWER QUESTIONS

Students should learn that if their notes list *people* or *things,* they can probably predict a short-answer question. Usually this kind of question requires only a couple of sentences or a paragraph at the most. Words like *list, name, define,* and *identify* are used by instructors when they ask a short-answer question.

To get an idea of how notes are used to predict short-answer questions, have students read over the two sets of notes shown in Figures 4.1 and 4.2 and the predicted short-answer question for each. (A form to use to help your students predict their own short-answer questions is provided in Appendix B.)

Figure 4.1

U.S. Government
1. Executive branch
a.   The president
b.   Executive departments
c.   Independent agencies
2. Legislative branch
a.   Senate
b.   House of Representatives
3. Judicial branch
a.   Supreme Court
b.   Other federal courts

Predicted short-answer question:
List the three branches of the U.S. government and identify what those branches include.

Figure 4.2   Animal Cells—Main Parts

1. *Membrane: Encloses the entire cell, holding it together.*
2. *Nucleus: The control center that directs activities of the cell.*
3. *Cytoplasm: All the cell except the nucleus—Proteins are made here and many of the cell's life activities take place here.*

Predicted short-answer question:
List the three main parts of the animal cell and define them.

TEST PREP: EXERCISE 4.1

Students are to go through the following sets of notes and predict a short-answer question for each, using words such as *list, name, define,* and *identify.* (Answers are in Appendix A.)

1.

Rules on Semicolon Usage
A semicolon is a punctuation mark.
A semicolon should be used to combine two closely related sentences.
A semicolon should be used to separate a series of phrases that are long or have punctuation, like commas, within them.
A semicolon should be used along with a conjunctive adverb and a comma to clarify the relationship between two closely related complete sentences.
Some examples of conjunctive adverbs include however, in addition, therefore, moreover, subsequently, consequently, additionally, and instead.

Predicted short-answer question:

_____

_____

_____

2.

Rules on Comma Usage
Use a comma to separate the elements in a series of three or more things, including the last two.
Use a comma and a conjunction such as and, but, for, nor, yet, or, or so to connect two independent clauses.

(Continued)

(Continued)

Use a comma to set off parenthetical elements or a part of a sentence that can be removed without changing the essential meaning of that sentence.
Use a comma to set off introductory elements.
Use a comma to separate coordinate adjectives.
Use a comma to set off phrases that express contrast.
Use a comma to set off quoted elements.
Use a comma to avoid confusion.
Use a comma for certain typographical reasons, such as between a city and a state, a date and the year, a name and a title when the title comes after the name, in long numbers, etc.

Predicted short-answer question:

_____

_____

_____

3.

Margaret Mitchell's "Gone With the Wind"
Main Characters and Their Traits:
Scarlett: vivacious, strong, optimistic, beautiful, life force of her family, primary character of novel
Ashley: dreamer, weak, ineffective, secondary male character, can't deal with the new life
Rhett: strong, handsome, devilish personality, realist, primary male character, opportunist
Melanie: gentle, represents goodness and decency, weak health, devotion and sweetness, secondary female character

Predicted short-answer question:

_____

_____

_____

4.

Late 19th-Century American Authors
1. Samuel Clemens (Mark Twain): Tom Sawyer, Huckleberry Finn, A Connecticut Yankee in King Arthur's Court
2. Edith Wharton: Ethan Frome, The Age of Innocence, The House of Mirth
3. Henry James: Daisy Miller, Portrait of a Lady, The Bostonian

Predicted short-answer question:

_____

_____

_____

LONG-ANSWER "TRACE" QUESTIONS

In a similar manner, students should learn that if their notes outline or describe steps of a process or the historical development of something, they can probably predict a "trace" question. Charts in textbooks or on handouts are also potential material for trace questions. Any of the following phrases signals a trace question:

- Describe the steps in . . .
- Trace the development of . . .
- Trace the events leading up to . . .
- Outline the history of . . .

Students should look through the sets of notes shown in Figures 4.3 and 4.4 and see how the trace questions were predicted. (A form for students to use to predict their own long-answer trace questions is provided in Appendix B.)

Figure 4.3

How RNA Is Formed
1. When RNA copies DNA's blueprint for making a protein, the DNA ladder first splits
lengthwise through its bases—half serves as a mold to form the messenger RNA.
2. Free RNA bases match up with attached sugars, and phosphates match up with exposed DNA bases.
3. It forms as the reverse of the DNA blueprint and peels off the DNA mold.
4. Halves of DNA start to rejoin.
5. Completed RNA strand leaves nucleus and goes to the ribosomes.

Predicted compare-and-contrast question:
Describe the steps in the formation of RNA.

Figure 4.4

Important Events Prior to the Revolutionary War
1763—Britain stationed a standing army in America and prohibited colonists from settling west
of the Appalachian Mts.
1765—Parliament passed the Stamp Act, taxing newspapers and legal documents in colonies.
1770—British troops killed American civilians in Boston Massacre.
1773—Colonists staged Boston Tea Party.
1774—The Intolerable Acts closed Boston Harbor to punish colonists.

Predicted compare-and-contrast question:
Trace the important events leading up to the Revolutionary War in America.

TEST PREP: EXERCISE 4.2

Students should go through the following sets of notes and predict a trace question for each, using one of the phrases listed on page 51. (Answers are in Appendix A.)

1.

Distribution of Product From Manufacturer

Predicted trace question:

_____

_____

_____

2.

Events Leading to Great Depression
1. Dust storms in Midwest caused hardship to farmers during the 1920s.
2. The stock market crashed in 1929.
3. Frightened stockholders sold out.
4. Banks collapsed and businesses folded.
5. People lost their jobs, their savings, and their homes.

Predicted compare-and-contrast question:

_____

_____

_____

_____

3.

Health Class — Exercising
1. It is important to warm up before exercising.
2. Warming up before exercise prevents injuries.
3. Allow five to ten minutes for a good warm-up.
4. First, do five minutes of walking.
5. Then, for two to three minutes, do some warm-up exercises specific to whatever sport you will be playing.
6. Last, for two to three minutes do some light stretching.

Predicted short-answer question:

_____

_____

_____

LONG-ANSWER "COMPARE AND CONTRAST" QUESTIONS

As above, if the student's notes describe two or more things that have some similar and some dissimilar characteristics, the student can usually predict a compare-and-contrast question. The following phrases usually signal a compare-and-contrast question.

- Tell how [two or more things] are alike or different.
- Weigh [or consider] the advantages or disadvantages of . . .
- Compare and contrast [two or more things].
- Show the similarities and differences between _____ and _____.

Have students look through the sets of notes in Figures 4.5 and 4.6 to see how the compare-and-contrast questions were predicted. (A form for students to use to predict their own compare-and-contrast questions is provided in Appendix B.)

Figure 4.5

Abraham Lincoln — 1860s	_John F. Kennedy — 1960s_
Rights of citizenship for blacks	_Equal rights for blacks_
Assassinated in office	_Assassinated in office_
First Republican President	_Democratic President_
More interested in national affairs	_Interested in both national and international affairs_
Self-educated, "plain folks," and poor	_Highly educated, socially prominent, and wealthy_
Became an American hero	_Became an American hero_

Predicted compare-and-contrast question:
Compare and contrast Presidents Lincoln and Kennedy.

Figure 4.6

Psychologist	Psychiatrist
1. Usually has MA or PhD degree with special training in psychology.	1. Has MD degree and special training in mental illness.
2. Deals with animal and human behavior—normal & abnormal.	2. Deals with abnormal human behavior.
3. Does not prescribe medication.	3. Can prescribe medication.

Predicted compare-and-contrast question:

Show the similarities and differences between the work and training of the psychologist and the psychiatrist.

TEST PREP: EXERCISE 4.3

Students should go through the following sets of notes and predict a compare-and-contrast question for each, using the phrases listed on page 53. (Answers are in Appendix A.)

1.

Ken Kesey's *One Flew Over the Cuckoo's Nest*—Main Characters and Their Traits	
1. Randle McMurphy	3. Chief
(institutionalized)	(institutionalized)
boisterous	silent
rebel	passive
fun-loving	strong
strong-willed	huge
not insane	probably not insane
feigns insanity for a softer life	feigns being insane and deaf and dumb to escape the cruelties of life
2. Nurse Ratched	
(runs institution)	
calm	
authoritarian	
disciplinarian	
tyrant	
insane with power	
feigns sanity	

Predicted trace question:

_____

_____

_____

2.

> Great 20th-Century American Artists
>
> Georgia O'Keeffe (from New Mexico): Painter of organic abstract forms in strong, clear colors; frequently employed Southwest motifs, as in Cow's Skull, Red, White, and Blue (1931).
>
> Louis Comfort Tiffany (from New York City): Creator of new art form—used freely shaped iridescent glass combined with metal; designer of jewelry & buildings, painter, decorator, glassmaker, and philanthropist; part of Art Nouveau movement (1890–1910, swept through Europe & America).
>
> Frank Lloyd Wright (from Midwest): Designed more than 600 buildings, including skyscrapers, factories, and private homes; main principle was "organic architecture" (building should suit its inhabitants & surroundings).

Predicted compare-and-contrast question:

_____

_____

_____

3.

> Latitude and Longitude
>
> Latitude
>
> • Shown as a horizontal line.
>
> • Is the angular distance of a point north or south of the equator.
>
> • Measured in degrees, minutes, and seconds.
>
> • Also called "parallels."
>
> Longitude
>
> • Shown as a vertical line.
>
> • Is the angular distance of a point east or west of the prime meridian.
>
> • Measured in degrees, minutes, and seconds.
>
> • Also called "meridians."

(Continued)

(Continued)

Predicted compare-and-contrast question:

_____

_____

_____

LONG-ANSWER "DISCUSS" QUESTIONS

Explain to your students that when their notes describe a specific individual, situation, or institution, they can usually expect a "discuss" question. The following phrases signal a discuss question:

- Discuss the significance or the problems of . . .
- What is the relationship between _____ and _____ ?
- Discuss the effect of . . .
- Discuss the role of . . .

Students are to look through the notes in Figures 4.7 and 4.8 and see how the discussion questions were predicted for each of them. (A form for students to use to predict their own "discussion" questions is provided in Appendix B.)

Figure 4.7

Effects of the Civil War
1. _Economy of the South was crippled._
2. _Republican Party gained control._
3. _Heritage of hate was left on both sides._
4. _Southern way of life ended._
5. _Gov't created more jobs during Reconstruction._
6. _Reconstruction period led to America's industrial era._

Predicted discussion question:
Discuss some of the effects of the Civil War in America.

Figure 4.8

Franchising

Parent company sells others the right to open similar business under its name and supplies market identification and know-how—makes big profits.

Franchisee pays a fee to parent company, buys supplies from franchiser, and increases the value of the parent company through reputation of each franchise—franchisee's profits are relatively smaller. Parent company runs risk because of big investments of money and chance of franchise getting a bad image.

Predicted discussion question:

What is the relationship between a parent company and its franchisee?

TEST PREP: EXERCISE 4.4

Have students go through the following sets of notes and predict a discussion question for each, using the phrases listed on page 56. (Answers are in Appendix A.)

1.

Greek Mythology

The Olympians are 12 immortal deities who lived in a palace on the top of Mount Olympus.

1. Ares was the god of war. He was beaten by Hercules in a battle and was almost killed by two giants who put him into a jar.

2. Apollo was the god of healing, music, and prophecy. He brought about the demise of Achilles.

3. Aphrodite was the goddess of love, fertility, and beauty. Some believe she was born from sea foam, and others say she was the daughter of Zeus and Dione.

4. Artemis was known as the virgin goddess of the hunt. She helped women who were going through childbirth.

5. Athena was the goddess of the arts and of war and was the patron goddess of Athens.

6. Demeter was the goddess of agriculture and crops. She was the sister of Zeus.

7. Dionysus was the god of wine and the son of Zeus.

8. Hephaestus of the lame god of fire, crafts, and blacksmiths. He was the son of Zeus and Hera, or perhaps Hera alone.

9. Hera was the wife of Zeus and the queen. She was the goddess of marriage.

10. Hermes was the guide of dead souls and was the messenger god. He was a prankster.

11. Poseidon was the god of the sea, horses, and earthquakes. He spent more time in the sea than on Mount Olympus.

12. Zeus was the head god of the Olympians.

(Continued)

(Continued)

Predicted trace question:

_____

_____

_____

2.

> _Hiroshima After the Bomb (1945)_
>
> _1. Approx. 350,000–400,000 people were vaporized by the searing heat in Hiroshima._
>
> _2. Approx. the same number died a short time after in terrible pain._
>
> _3. (a) A third group lived but suffered wounds, burns, mental anguish, and massive doses of_
>
> _radiation (weak, sick to stomachs, loss of hair, changes to cell structure caused cancer,_
>
> _genetic defects in children)._
>
> _(b) Many of these survivors fled Hiroshima after bombing and went to Nagasaki_
>
> _(200 mi. SW) and were killed in a second atomic bomb blast._

Predicted trace question:

_____

_____

_____

3.

> _Jim Crow Laws (in segregationist and civil rights movements)_
>
> _In 1828, Thomas Dartmouth Rice appeared onstage during a minstrel show with_
>
> _blackened face, old clothes, and sang song ident. himself as "Jim Crow." Characterization_
>
> _became a popular stereotype of the black man among racist whites. Whites saw in Jim_
>
> _Crow a black man who had the status they thought he deserved in a white society. Laws_
>
> _were passed after Civil War in the South to try to keep blacks "in their place," or segregated,_
>
> _from whites. These laws became known as Jim Crow laws. Groups like the Ku Klux Klan_
>
> _enforced them. Laws stemming from these were the grandfather clause and the poll tax_
>
> _(prohibited by the Voting Rights Act). The attitudes expressed by Jim Crow laws proved to be_
>
> _more difficult to eradicate than the laws themselves._

Predicted trace question:

_____

_____

_____

PRACTICING ANSWERS

Once students have looked over their test analysis forms, organized their notes, and predicted the probable essay questions, have them practice answering the questions using their notes. Following are some tips to give students for answering essay questions:

1. Begin by turning the question into a statement.

2. List or state each point or idea clearly. Take care that the ideas do not run together. It can be helpful to outline the answer first.

3. Because neatness and organization can affect how many points an instructor will give for their answers, it is a good idea for students to practice writing with care so that organization and clear handwriting will come more naturally when they take the test. Students who are not sure if their handwriting can be clearly read might ask a friend or family member to look over their answers to get some feedback. Some students should print their answers.

4. Students ought to be encouraged to consider the predicted questions and practice answers as a dress rehearsal for their tests. Saving their practice answers to read over just before tests will help them keep the content fresh in their memory.

Before students practice writing essay answers, review the example in Figure 4.9. It can help you demonstrate the use of the above tips.

Predicted question:

Name the main characters in Gone with the Wind and give their traits.

Answer:

Figure 4.9

The main characters in Gone with the Wind are Scarlett, Rhett, Ashley, and Melanie.

Scarlett, the primary character of the novel, is vivacious, strong, optimistic, beautiful,

and the life force of her family. Rhett, the primary male character, is strong and

handsome, with a devilish personality. Rhett is a realist and opportunist. Ashley, the

secondary male character, is a dreamer. He proves to be weak and ineffective and

can't deal with the new life he's forced to live. Melanie, the secondary female character, is

gentle, devoted, and sweet. Her health is weak. Melanie represents goodness and decency.

TEST PREP: EXERCISE 4.5

Students should practice writing essay answers to some of the questions they predicted earlier in the chapter.

1. Rules on semicolon usage (Test Prep: Exercise 4.1)

Predicted question:

_____

_____

Answer:

_____

_____

_____

_____

_____

_____

_____

_____

_____

_____

2. Rules on comma usage (Test Prep: Exercise 4.1)

Predicted question:

_____

_____

Answer:

_____

_____

_____

_____

_____

_____

_____

_____

_____

_____

_____

3. Late-19th-century American authors (Test Prep: Exercise 4.1)

Predicted question:

_____

_____

Answer:

_____

_____

_____

_____

_____

_____

_____

_____

_____

_____

_____

_____

4. Distribution of product from manufacturer (Test Prep: Exercise 4.2)

Predicted question:

_____

_____

Answer:

_____

_____

_____

_____

_____

_____

_____

_____

_____

_____

_____

_____

(Continued)

(Continued)

5. Great 20th-century American artists (Test Prep: Exercise 4.3)

Predicted question:

_____

_____

Answer:

_____

_____

_____

_____

_____

_____

_____

_____

_____

_____

_____

6. Hiroshima after the bomb (Test Prep: Exercise 4.4)

Predicted question:

_____

_____

Answer:

_____

_____

_____

_____

_____

_____

_____

_____

_____

_____

IMPROVING ANSWERS WITH LIBRARY RESEARCH

An important learning tool to share with your students is how to enrich their study notes with citations, statistics, and other information from authorities on a particular topic by using the reference resources in the library. Citing references or pieces of information on an essay test shows that a student has done extra outside reading or research on a topic that might have been suggested by a teacher. Citing the name of one or two authorities and their articles can be enough to let a teacher know that a student has made a special effort to study. Even better, however, is for students to skim the articles at the library or on the Internet and take down a few important names and facts to use in their essay answers; they can group this information with their other study notes on the topic.

The library has both electronic and print guides and indexes to various types of periodical literature, books, newspapers, documents, and surveys that can be used to identify the most current authors, articles, and statistics on all kinds of topics. You can familiarize your students with how to practice researching a topic or a famous person by having them follow the steps below at your school library. (A form for students to use to practice researching a topic is provided in Appendix B.)

Researching a Topic

Choose a topic to research.

Write it here. _____

1. Research the topic or person on programs available on your library's computers or in appropriate printed indexes. Start with broad reference sources, including encyclopedias, bibliographies, and indexes, which can be found by accessing your library's catalog. Ask your librarian to suggest some specific resources appropriate to your topic as well as descriptors, or key words, for your search.

Name of Periodical	Name of Article	Author	Date	Vol.	Pages
(1)					
(2)					
(3)					

2. Find one of the articles listed above and skim through it for two or three important facts (for example, the date of an important discovery or event, the name of an important person and her contribution, an important idea or concept and the name of the responsible person).

(1) _____

(2) _____

(3) _____

Researching Statistics

Use the current *Statistical Abstract of the United States* or find even more up-to-date statistics for your topic above by using an online resource such as Statistical Universe. (The *Statistical Abstract* is published once a year by the U.S. Department of Commerce, Bureau of the Census; it is a national data book citing current statistics on a comprehensive range of trends, subjects, and topics.) Statistical Universe, an electronic database that provides abstracts and locator information for all statistical reports of general research value, is also issued by the federal government. Consult your librarian for relevant descriptors if you have trouble finding your topic. Cite three statistics relevant to your topic and list the sources for those statistics. (A form for students to use to practice researching statistics is provided in Appendix B.)

Statistic	Source, or Survey Done By	Date
(1)		
(2)		
(3)		

Researching a Famous Person

Choose a famous person to research.

Write the name of the person here: _____

1. Use *Current Biography* or an electronic resource, such as Biography Resource Center, to find accurate biographical information and articles. Consult the librarian to find out what biographical reference works are available in your library. Find three sources (articles or books) in one of these indexes and provide the information below. (A form for students to use to practice researching a famous person is provided in Appendix B.)

Source (name of book, article, or periodical)	Author	Date	Pages
(1)			
(2)			
(3)			

2. Find one of the sources listed above and skim through it for two or three important facts about the person.

   (1) _____

   (2) _____

   (3) _____

TEST PREP: EXERCISE 4.6

Students can practice answering an essay question, using both study notes and notes from library research. Below are some notes on the trends in U.S. population mobility and its causes. Following the notes are some library citations and statistics marked with an (*). Students should answer the predicted question using all the notes and library citations.

Causes of Current Mobility Trends in Urban U.S.

1. *Change of lifestyle—caused by changes in family structure, inflation, need for self-fulfillment*

2. *Change of economic base—caused by changes in family structure, job change, education, transfers in jobs (many businesses are moving away from metro area because of inflation)*

3. *Rising inflation—affecting transportation (high cost of cars, gas) and desire for public transportation (more economical); cost of housing (housing closer to metro is often more costly, while housing further out—even outside suburbs—is often more reasonable)*

4. *Back-to-nature movement (move to country) and back-to-culture movement (move closer to metro life and advantages of big city—restore slum and old areas and live there)*

    * *Between 1950 and 1960, 1.1% of overall population moved into the central city.*

    * *Between 1950 and 1960, 3.8% of overall population moved outside the central city.*

    * *Between 1960 and 1970, 0.6% of overall population moved into the central city.*

    * *Between 1960 and 1970, 2.4% of overall population moved outside central city.*

    * *1970–1978, 0.6% moved into central city.*

    * *1970–1978, 1.5% moved outside central city.*

(Statistics from U.S. Bureau of the Census of Population and Current Population Reports)

Predicted question:

Discuss the causes of the current mobility trends in the urban United States.

Outline:

(Continued)

Answer:

_____

_____

_____

CHAPTER SUMMARY

Learning how to prepare for taking essay tests means not only that students can organize, condense, and memorize their notes, as covered in Chapter 3, but that they can also predict and practice answering essay questions. Students can usually predict from their notes what kind of questions they will be asked—short-answer questions (list, define, identify) or long-answer questions (trace, compare-and-contrast, discuss). Adding source citations and facts from library research about test topics will undoubtedly help to bolster their scores. Even if the questions they predict are not exactly the same as those on the test, just the process of predicting questions and practicing answers will in and of itself help students get to know the material thoroughly—it will make them more *prepared* students.

5

Preparing for Objective Questions and Tests

While essay tests require subjective judgment by the grader, there is only one correct way to answer multiple-choice, matching, true/false, and completion questions. The answers are marked right or wrong according to an answer key, and no matter who corrects the test, the results are the same.

Taking an objective test (except for completion questions and some true/false questions) requires the student to recognize the right answer rather than recall it from one's memory bank. As noted in Chapter 3, recognition is easier than recall. Consequently, a student can generally get by with a less thorough knowledge of a subject than is needed for essay tests. People who are already familiar with a topic can even sometimes pass an objective test about it without studying especially for the test; however, this familiarity with a topic can only be gained by studying the course content. Additionally, research shows that students who prepare for objective tests as thoroughly as they do for essay tests score higher than students who have prepared only enough to recognize the right answers.

Studying for an objective test requires following the steps in Chapter 3: organize class notes and reading, make study notes on each topic, condense those notes, memorize them, and review them over and over. Students should also try to predict test questions using notes and a test analysis form. Preparing for an objective test requires putting less time into practicing answers than is needed for an essay test: In making up an objective question, the student already knows exactly what the answer should be. Students may find it helpful, nevertheless, to spend some study time with a group to practice answering each other's predicted questions.

In this chapter, students will learn how to make multiple-choice, matching, true/false, and completion questions from their study notes. Even though it is unlikely they will predict the exact questions on a given test, they will at least become familiar with the material through the process of predicting questions from study notes.

PRACTICING MULTIPLE-CHOICE QUESTIONS

Multiple-choice questions present the test taker with a choice from among three, four, or five possible answers. The questions consist of a stem (also called a lead or an introduction) followed by the possible answers (also called alternatives). All the alternatives may be so different that the right choice is obvious, or they may be quite similar and require more careful consideration.

To demonstrate how study notes can be turned into multiple-choice questions, have students read through the study notes shown in Figure 5.1 and the two multiple-choice questions predicted from those notes. (A form for students to use to predict their own multiple-choice questions is provided in Appendix B.)

Figure 5.1

John Steinbeck's *The Grapes of Wrath*
First published in 1939—America was still getting over the Great Depression.
A powerful dramatization of the forced migration of people from their bank-foreclosed farms in the Dust Bowl.
A dramatization of the plight of the dispossessed everywhere.
A great social document of an era in American history.
Main characters were the Joad family—"Okie" farmers.

Predicted Multiple-Choice Questions:

1. Which one of the following statements is NOT true about *The Grapes of Wrath*?
A. It portrays the plight of the dispossessed.
B. It is a great social document dramatizing the forced migration of people.
C. It takes place during World War II in the United States.
D. The main characters were a family of "Okie" farmers.
2. *The Grapes of Wrath* is a book about
A. the Joad family, who owned a vineyard in California during the Great Depression.
B. the Sartoris family, who moved from Oklahoma to California during the Great Depression.
C. the Joad family, who moved from the Dust Bowl to California during World War II.
D. the Joad family, whose plight represents that of the dispossessed everywhere.
Answers: 1. C; 2. D

TEST PREP: EXERCISE 5.1

Using some sample class notes about angles and the different types of angles, students are to predict a multiple-choice question on each set of notes and answer each of their predicted questions where indicated.

1.

Angles
Definition of "angle" —An angle is the union of two rays that have the same endpoint.
The sides of an angle are always called the two rays.
The vertex is the common endpoint of the rays.
Angles are measured in degrees.
The number of degrees tells you how wide the angle is.

Predicted multiple-choice question on "angles":

Stem: _____
       _____

A. _____
   _____

B. _____
   _____

C. _____
   _____

D. _____
   _____

Answer: _____

2.

Types of Angles
Zero angle—A single ray going toward the right
Acute angle—An angle that measures between zero and 90 degrees
Right angle—An angle with a measure of exactly 90 degees
Obtuse angle—An angle with a measure of greater than 90 degrees to 180 degrees
Straight angle—An angle with a measure of exactly 180 degrees

Predicted multiple-choice question on "types of angles":

Stem: _____
       _____

A. _____
   _____

(Continued)

(Continued)

B. _____

C. _____

D. _____

Answer: _____

3. Using the sample class notes from Chapter 4 (Figure 4.3) about RNA, students should predict a multiple-choice question and then answer it.

Predicted multiple-choice question based on "how RNA is formed":

Stem: _____

A. _____

B. _____

C. _____

D. _____

Answer: _____

4. Using the sample class notes from Chapter 4 on the Great Depression (Test Prep: Exercise 4.2), students should predict a multiple-choice question and then answer it.

Predicted multiple-choice question based on "events leading to the Great Depression":

Stem: _____

A. _____

B. _____

C. _____

D. _____

Answer: _____

PRACTICING MATCHING QUESTIONS

Matching questions are easy for students to make up because they do not need to think up alternatives to the right answer. They simply make a list of stems, or leads, and a list of correct answers to complete them—in a different order. To make a matching question harder, students can add more possible answers in the second column than there are stems in the first.

To see how a matching question is made from study notes, have students read through the notes on the novels *Babbitt* and *The Big Money* (Figure 5.2) and the notes and predicted multiple-choice questions above from *The Grapes of Wrath* (Figure 5.1). (A form for students to use to predict their own matching questions is provided in Appendix B.)

Figure 5.2

<u>Babbitt</u> by Sinclair Lewis
<u>Published in 1922.</u>
<u>Babbitt, a conniving and prosperous real estate man, is the main character.</u>
<u>Portrays total conformist.</u>
<u>Aspires for power in his community and self-esteem.</u>
<u>Is so filled with rationalizations that he doesn't recognize his own corruption.</u>
<u>A hardened and professional social climber.</u>

<u>The Big Money</u> by John Dos Passos
<u>Published in 1937.</u>
One of the "U.S.A." trilogy, which also includes <u>The 42nd Parallel</u> and <u>1919.</u>
<u>The classic novel of the "lost generation" of the 1920s.</u>
<u>The "lost generation" includes actresses, aviators, flappers, the Fords, and social workers.</u>
<u>Charley Anderson—Characterized by money making, murder, speakeasies, dreams, and delusions.</u>
<u>Main characters are:</u>   <u>Charley Anderson</u>—Simple aviator hero
<u>Mary French</u>—Loved humanity
<u>Marge Dowling</u>—Became the nation's sweetheart on the silver screen
<u>Dick Savage</u>—Public relations expert who climbed to power and self-destruction

---

(Continued)

Figure 5.2 (Continued)

Match the information with the appropriate novel. More than one of the descriptions in column 2 may apply to a novel.	
Column 1	Column 2
1. The Grapes of Wrath	A. Is a classic novel about "lost generation" of 1920s
2. Babbitt	B. Portrays the total conformist.
3. The Big Money	C. Portrays the plight of the dispossessed.
	D. Main characters are poor farmers.
	E. Main characters are actress, aviator, money maker, and social worker.
	F. Main character is a corrupt social climber.

Answers: 1. C, D; 2. B, F; 3. A, E

TEST PREP: EXERCISE 5.2

1. Using these sample class notes on "Staying Healthy," students should predict and then answer a matching question.

Staying Healthy
Being fit means eating well, getting a lot of physical exercise, drinking lots of water, and maintaining a healthy weight.
When you are fit, you feel good and can do all the things you want to do.
Some ways to stay fit include eating a variety of foods, including fruits and vegetables; drinking water and milk; limiting the amount of time you spend in front of the television or on the computer; and playing sports and other outdoor activities.
Some examples of healthy foods: fruits, vegetables, low-fat cheese, whole wheat bread, pasta, whole grain cereals.

Predicted matching question based on "staying healthy":

Answers: _____

2. Using the sample class notes from Chapter 4 about the U.S. government (Figure 4.1), students should predict a matching question and then answer it.

Predicted matching question based on "U.S. government":

Answers: _____

3. Using the sample class notes from Chapter 4 about the novel _One Flew Over the Cuckoo's Nest_ (Test Prep: Exercise 4.3), students should predict a matching question and then answer it.

Predicted matching question based on Ken Kesey's "_One Flew Over the Cuckoo's Nest_—Main Characters and Their Traits":

Answers: _____

PRACTICING TRUE/FALSE QUESTIONS

True/false questions (which can also be yes-no or right-wrong questions) test a student's knowledge of the material and his ability to read carefully and critically. Some statements are obviously true or obviously false. But a statement can also be mixed; that is, part of it may be true and part of it false—which means the entire statement should be marked false. True/false questions can also be made more difficult by asking for an explanation of why a statement is false; this explanation may be written out, or the word or phrase that makes the statement false may be underlined.

Here are two examples of true/false questions (Figure 5.3) based on the study notes from *The Grapes of Wrath* (Figure 5.1) and two based on the following set of notes on recycling (Figure 5.4). (A form for students to use to predict their own true/false questions is provided in Appendix B.)

Figure 5.3

Predicted True/False Questions:

1. *The Grapes of Wrath* was first published long after the Great Depression.
True or False?
2. In *The Grapes of Wrath*, the Joad family moved to the Dust Bowl.
True or False? If false, explain why.
Answers: 1. False; 2. False, because the Joad family moved from the Dust Bowl to California

Figure 5.4

Recycling
• There are many materials that can be recycled.
• Recycling is important because it allows new products to be made from items that would otherwise wind up in a landfill.
• New soda cans can be made out of recycled aluminum cans and aluminum foil.
• Paper can be made from old paper, which is recycled by shredding it into tiny bits and mixing it with water.

Predicted True/False Questions:

1. *It is better for the earth for companies to make new soda cans out of aluminum, rather than recycling old cans.*
True or False? Explain why.
2. *Paper is recycled by shredding it into tiny pieces and mixing it with water.*
True or False?
Answers: *1. False, because metals are easier for companies to recover and reuse rather than to mine new metal from the earth; 2. True*

TEST PREP: EXERCISE 5.3

Using these sample class notes on "perpendicular lines" and "parallel lines," students are to predict a true/false question for each topic.

1.

Perpendicular Lines
Perpendicular lines are two line segments in the same plane.
The two line segments must make a 90-degree angle.
If two lines in the same plane are each perpendicular to the same line, then those two lines are parallel to each other.

Predicted true/false question on "perpendicular lines":

_____

_____

Answer: _____

2.

Parallel Lines
Parallel lines are two lines in the same place.
Parallel lines never intersect.
Parallel lines always have the same distance between them.

(Continued)

(Continued)

Predicted true/false question on "perpendicular lines":

_____

_____

_____

Answer: _____

3. Using the sample class notes from Chapter 4 about cell structure (Figure 4.2) and franchising (Figure 4.8), students should predict a true/false question for each topic.

Predicted true/false question based on "animal cells—main parts":

_____

_____

_____

Answer: _____

Predicted true/false question based on "franchising":

_____

_____

_____

Answer: _____

PRACTICING COMPLETION QUESTIONS

Completion, or fill-in-the-blank, questions are the most difficult kind of objective questions because they require free-association answers: Students must fill in the blanks by recalling information in their memory banks. There are usually no alternatives to choose from. (A simpler kind of completion question asks the test taker to fill in the blank from a list of alternatives, which makes it essentially a multiple-choice question—but this kind of completion question is more common in the lower grades than in high school or college.) To answer completion questions, students may need to memorize entire definitions, theorems, laws, or passages.

Even though completion questions are the hardest kind of objective questions to answer, they are probably the easiest to construct. Here are two examples of predicted completion questions (Figure 5.5) based on the notes from _The Big Money_ (Figure 5.2) and two based on notes on rain forests (Figure 5.6). (A form for students to use to predict their own completion questions is provided in Appendix B.)

Figure 5.5

Predicted Completion Questions:

1. *The Big Money is the classic novel of* _____ *of the 1920s.*

2. _____ *is the aviator hero in The Big Money.*

Answers: 1. the "lost generation"; 2. Charley Anderson

Figure 5.6

Rain forests

Rain forests cover 2 percent of the earth's surface.

There are many plants and animals on earth.

Over half of the plant and animal species on the earth live in the rain forests.

Predicted Completion Questions:

1. *Rain forests cover* _____ *of the earth's surface.*

2. *Of all the plant and animal species on the earth,* _____ *live in the rain forests.*

Answers: 1. 2 percent; 2. over half

TEST PREP: EXERCISE 5.4

Using the sample class notes from Chapter 4 about the American Revolution (Figure 4.4) and Jim Crow laws (Test Prep: Exercise 4.4), predict a completion question for each topic.

1. **Predicted completion question based on "important events prior to the Revolutionary War":**

_____

_____

Answer: _____

2. **Predicted completion question based on "Jim Crow laws":**

_____

_____

Answer: _____

GROUP STUDY FOR OBJECTIVE TESTS

Because it is no challenge for students to answer the objective questions they made from their own study notes, it can be helpful for them to study with a group and test each other with predicted questions (Gettinger & Seibert, 2002; Johnson, 2006; Kuo, Hagie, & Miller, 2004; Petress, 2004). By taking someone else's predicted test, students can practice answering objective questions and identify information they need to review on their own (using the techniques in Chapter 4).

While group study can be an excellent way for students to prepare for an objective test, they should not limit themselves to that. They should plan for individual study time as well. To help them get the most out of group study for an objective test, here are some pointers you might emphasize:

1. Carefully select group members; they should be people who are well prepared and not likely to try to distract the group.

2. Agree before your study session to each prepare a set of predicted questions based on your study notes; it might be a good idea to decide how many kinds of questions you each will do, too.

3. At your study session, exchange the tests you have each written so everyone has a copy of all the tests done by everyone else in the group.

4. Take the practice tests one at a time and have the writer of one test read the correct answers before going on to the next test. If there are questions about any answers, discuss them before going on to another test. You may find it necessary to refer to your study notes to verify a disputed answer.

STANDARDIZED TESTS

Standardized tests are commercially developed tests designed to assess knowledge of certain topics or subjects, and they are administered under very prescribed and uniform conditions. Students will undoubtedly encounter a number of these standardized tests during their academic careers—whether the Scholastic Aptitude Test (SAT), the high-school equivalency exam (GED), or one of the many kinds of qualifying exams required for entry into a profession, a college, or a graduate school in a particular field.

Standardized tests by and large come in two varieties—norm referenced and criterion referenced, and these differ on how the test results are reported. On a norm-referenced test, the examinee's score is expressed as a comparison with how others have scored on the same test; a 50 percent score means that half the test takers scored higher and half scored lower.

With criterion-referenced tests, on the other hand, the score expresses how successfully a test taker met the objectives from which the test was developed; a 50 percent score in this case means that half the questions were answered correctly.

The preparation for both kinds of standardized tests is the same. Your students should be as well read in the subject as possible. Study guides may be available at the bookstore, in your school library, or on the Internet for the test, or the test developer may furnish objectives or a description of the test content. Although the test-taking cues described in Chapter 8 will still be highly useful, successfully eliminating the incorrect alternatives in multiple-choice questions—the most common kind of objective questions on standardized tests—is much likelier when a student is familiar with the subject matter.

CHAPTER SUMMARY

Predicting questions for objective tests is a useful way for students to gain familiarity with the material. If they know the test will have multiple-choice, matching, true/false, or fill-in-the-blank questions, those are the types of questions they should make up from their notes. Extensively reviewing their notes (using the study techniques from Chapter 3), anticipating questions indicated as test topics, and using the information on their test analysis forms are logical ways students can study for an objective exam. Exchanging and taking practice exams with a small group of classmates can also prove a beneficial way to spend some of their study time.

PART THREE

Taking Tests and Doing Better

6

Getting It Together on Test Day

The day of the exam: the day when a student's preparations will (hopefully) pay off! Review the following steps with your students to ensure they will be as organized for the test as possible.

ON THE WAY

1. *Gather all the necessary materials.* Before leaving for the test, be sure you have your condensed notes, pens, sharpened pencils with erasers, plenty of clean paper, and a wristwatch. Allow enough time to get all of these items together. If your instructor prefers a certain type of paper or exam booklet, or a certain color of pencil or ink, have the right kind ready. Also, take along any special instruments you will need, such as a ruler or calculator.

2. *Wear comfortable clothes and shoes.* You want to be relaxed and able to concentrate fully on the test.

3. *Psych yourself up for the test.* Review your reasons from Chapter 1 for doing well on it.

4. *Leave a little early* so you'll have about 15 minutes after you arrive at the test room before the test starts. If you have to rush to get to the test, you'll make yourself unnecessarily anxious.

5. When you arrive at the test room, find a quiet place before going in to *review and recite any notes* that must be memorized verbatim. Then put your notes away and do not take them out again until after you finish the test.

IN THE TEST ROOM

6. Walk into the test room about five or ten minutes early and find *a seat where you will be comfortable* (if seats are not already assigned). Some students prefer sitting in the back row; others, in the front. Whatever your preference, sit where you will have plenty of elbow room and no one close enough to distract you during the test.

7. While waiting for the exam to be distributed, *get your pens, pencils, and other materials out and ready.* Organize them on the top of your desk.

8. If you are becoming anxious, *practice some of the relaxation techniques* from Chapter 1.

BEFORE STARTING TO ANSWER

9. Your teacher or the test proctor will give out the tests and direct you to write the answers on the test, your own paper, or an answer sheet or exam booklet. *Listen carefully to all directions.* If you are confused about any of them, immediately raise your hand and ask for clarification.

10. *Write your name and other required identifying information* on the test or the answer sheet. Do not waste time supplying unnecessary information. For example, some teachers use machine-scorable answer sheets for objective exams, which often have blanks for age, date of birth, name of school, and so on. If your teacher asks you to furnish only your name and the date, then ignore the other blanks.

11. *Jot down memorized facts.* As soon as the teacher has given directions and the test has officially begun, write down all the names, dates, formulas, or theorems you reviewed just before entering the test room as well as any other facts from your study notes that come to mind immediately. This will take a minute or two of test time but will be well worth it because you will not risk forgetting these facts while you look over the test. And you will have them at hand when you need them to answer a question. Do not begin to jot these facts down until the exam has officially started, however; you do not want there to be any question about the possibility of cheating.

12. *Position the exam so you won't have to cross your arm over your line of vision to record each answer.* If you are right-handed, put the exam on the left side of the desk and the answer sheet on the right. If you are left-handed, put the exam on the right side of the desk and the answer sheet on the left.

13. *Assess the exam.* Quickly look it over from beginning to end to get a sense of the number and type of questions and their point values.

14. *Make a schedule for completing the test*. Because you want to give yourself the chance to answer all the questions to which you know the answers, you need to pace yourself. If you spend too much time on a difficult question, you might not have time left to answer easier ones that come after it. The kind of schedule you will make for an essay test is somewhat different from that for an objective test, and both kinds will be explained in Chapters 7 and 8. But whichever kind of test you are taking, you should allow time to go through it once answering all the questions that are easy for you. Then go back a second time to complete the more difficult questions and do a final check for careless errors and omissions.

15. If at any time during the test, you find yourself tensing up, take a minute and *do some of the relaxation exercises* described in Chapter 1 so you will be able to concentrate on the test.

CHAPTER SUMMARY

A student taking a test wants to be able to concentrate on turning the information studied into correct answers. There are a thousand little distractions, but these can be kept to a minimum if the student goes in organized. This means making sure to have all the necessary test-taking materials—from pencils to exam booklets—before going to take the test; it also means allowing ample time to get to the test room and quickly review important memorized facts before actually going in to sit down.

Once in the test room, students should look for seats allowing them plenty of elbow room, where others taking the test will not distract them. Other pointers to observe after the test is handed out are to make sure they understand the directions, jot down all the facts they have memorized for the test, and make a game plan that will afford them the best opportunity possible to answer every question.

7

Taking the Essay Test

Because essay questions require recall memory rather than just recognition, students should be aware that instructors use them to evaluate how *thoroughly* students have mastered course material. Consequently, essay questions require more in the way of preparation: not just very thorough study but also the ability to provide complete, well organized, clear, neat answers.

Form is also important. Essay tests are graded more subjectively than objective tests, and there is not just one simple way to answer each question. Although most teachers have an answer key that lists the concepts and facts they think the ideal answers should contain, the student's grade depends on an ability to communicate those concepts and facts to the teacher. Essays that are incomplete, that weave back and forth from point to point, that don't directly answer the question, or that are hard to read give the teacher the impression that the student doesn't know the material.

A student who has studied as outlined in Chapters 3 and 4 should know the material thoroughly. This chapter will deal with how students can communicate that knowledge on an essay test. The student's goal, ultimately, is to answer all essay questions as thoroughly, clearly, and concisely as possible. To do that, students will need to understand how to budget their time, the importance of addressing an essay specifically to the question asked, and how to write their answer in a neat, organized manner.

BUDGETING TIME

After they have gotten the test and unloaded the facts from their memories, students should quickly look over the exam to see how many questions they will have to answer and how many points each is worth. For example, they may be asked to answer two out of three or one out of two from each section, or three out of five from the entire test. They should try to ascertain whether the questions in one section are worth more than the questions in another. If the test does not indicate the point value of the questions, they should immediately ask the teacher.

As the students read through the test, certain questions will seem easier to answer than others. They should choose now the questions they will answer. As they read, concepts and facts to include in their answer may occur to them, and they should note them as they go through the test. These should be one- or two-word notes to jog the memory and to return to later when writing out the answers.

Following their assessment of how many questions there are and how much each is worth, students should plan a schedule, allowing time to read each question carefully, outline the answers, and make a final check for careless omissions and errors.

For an example of how a student might budget time for a 55-minute essay test that has three equally weighted questions, look at Figure 7.1. At least five minutes should be spent assessing the test, choosing questions, and making a schedule, with the last four or five minutes of the test period allotted for a final check and about ten minutes before that for re-reading answers to make sure they are complete. These three steps will use up 19 or 20 minutes, leaving 35 or 36 minutes to answer the questions. So, assuming three equally weighted questions, the student should spend 12 minutes on each question—2 or 3 minutes on an outline and the remaining 9 or 10 minutes writing out the answer.

If some questions are worth more points than others, students should adjust their schedule to spend more time on the question or questions that are worth more points. For example, if there are three questions and one is worth twice as much as each of the other two, twice as much time should be spent on that question.

READING THE QUESTION CAREFULLY

You should make sure your students are aware that their essay must fit the question. If the teacher asks them to *analyze* an event, a simple description

Figure 7.1

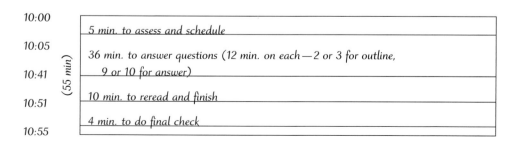

of it will not do. A question that asks the student to *interpret* a poem cannot be answered just by summarizing the poem.

Chapter 4 dealt with learning to use notes to help students predict the kinds of essay questions they're likely to face—short-answer questions or long-answer trace, compare-and-contrast, or discussion questions. This section features some of the "exam words" used to signal those different types of questions and the appropriate kind of essay answer to write for each. Have students first read carefully through the words and the corresponding answer descriptions under "Essay Exam Terms" below. Then have them practice applying these by doing Test Prep: Exercise 7.1.

Essay Exam Terms

Short-Answer Terms

Classify. Group the information in a diagram, chart, or description according to its main parts or characteristics.

Define. Give concise, clear, and authoritative meaning. Don't give details but do make sure you have given a complete definition. Show how the thing you are defining differs from things in other classifications, if necessary.

Diagram. Make a drawing, chart, plan, or other graphic answer. Label the information in it. It is a good idea to add a brief explanation or description.

Enumerate. Write in a list or in an outline form. Give points concisely and one by one.

Give an example. Cite one instance or one situation to support the general point.

Illustrate. Use a picture, diagram, or concrete example to explain or clarify.

List. Write an itemized series of concise statements, giving names, things, or points one by one. Make a list of all the important names or components.

State. Present the main points in a brief, clear sequence, usually omitting details, illustrations, or examples.

Summarize. Give the main points or facts in a condensed form, omitting small details or examples.

Long-Answer Trace Terms

Describe. Recount or relate in sequence the steps requested. (Note: This can also be a short-answer signal if a single thing, rather than a sequence, is to be described; then you would characterize or sketch the thing in expository form.)

Outline. Organize a description under main points and subordinate points, stressing the process or relationship among events. (Note: This can also be a short-answer signal if a single thing, rather than a sequence, is to be outlined;

in that case, omit minor details and use the outline to describe or classify.)

Trace. In narrative form, describe a process, development, steps, or historical events.

Long-Answer Compare-and-Contrast Terms

Compare. Emphasize the similarities between two (or more) things and, in some cases, also mention the differences.

Contrast. Stress the differences between objects, ideas, qualities, characteristics, events, or concepts.

Relate. Show how things are connected to each other or how one thing causes another, correlates with another, or is similar to another.

Long-Answer Discussion Terms

Analyze. Carefully appraise the situation or problem, citing both advantages and limitations. Emphasize your personal evaluation in light of the appraisal of authorities you have noted.

Criticize. Express your judgment about the merit or truth of the factors, concepts, or views mentioned. Give the results of your analysis of them, discussing their strong points and limitations.

Defend. Present one side of an argument, issue, or situation. If you can, cite the views of authorities or some data to support your side.

Discuss. Examine, analyze carefully, and give the reasons and all relevant details about a specific situation, individual, or institution. Be as complete and detailed as possible.

Evaluate. Carefully appraise the problem or situation, citing both advantages and limitations. Emphasize the appraisal of authorities and, to a lesser degree, your personal appraisal.

Explain. Interpret, clarify, and carefully spell out the material you present. Give reasons for differences of opinion or of results. Try to analyze the causes of the differences.

Interpret. Translate, give examples of, solve, or comment on a subject. Give your judgment about it in light of all you know about it.

Justify. Prove or give reasons for decisions or conclusions. Strive to be convincing. Cite authorities or data to support your position.

Prove. Establish that something is true by citing factual evidence or giving clear, logical reasoning.

Review. Examine a subject critically, analyzing and commenting on the important information about it.

TEST PREP: EXERCISE 7.1

Students can check their knowledge of the terms described above by reading each of the descriptions below and, on the blank line following, writing the term that the teacher should use in wording the essay question. In some cases, more than one word will fit the question. (Answers are in the back of the book in Appendix A.)

1. In a course on the U.S. government, the teacher wants students to think over the functions and responsibilities of the navy and the army and bring out the points of difference. Which term should be used in the question?

   _____

   _____

2. The instructor in an American history class mentions a body of water in the possession of the enemy in wartime. A plan is proposed for retaking it. If students are to express their judgments of the merits of the plan, which term should be used in the question?

   _____

   _____

3. When and where did the American justice system have its beginning? What has been the general history of its development? The history teacher wants students to follow the course of its progress. Which term should be used?

   _____

   _____

4. Which term should a world history teacher use to ask for a concrete example of the use of submarines in World War II?

   _____

   _____

5. In an art course, the teacher has discussed the experimental work of Cézanne, Van Gogh, and others. On a written examination, students are asked to pick out the main points of discussion and bring them together in a concise overall statement. Which term should be used in the question?

   _____

   _____

6. In a chemistry class, the teacher wants students to make clear the nature of a chemical-bond reaction, particularly how it comes about. Which term should be used in the question?

   _____

   _____

(Continued)

(Continued)

7. In an economics class, the teacher has lectured on the decontrol of oil and gas prices. On the test, students will need to think over the topic and consider it from various points of view. They will be asked to present different sides of the issue. Which term should be used in the question?

_____

_____

8. In an English course, the teacher has assigned a term paper and has told students how to proceed in collecting the necessary material. On a quiz, they will have to give the steps briefly, one after another. Which term should be used?

_____

_____

9. In a geology class, the teacher has used television to show that cross-bedding is a common feature of sandstones. On a quiz, the teacher wants to be sure that students really know the meaning of the term *cross-bedding*. Which term should be used in the question?

_____

_____

10. A literature teacher wants students to consider the ways in which early French, Spanish, and English literature are alike and the ways in which they are different. Which term should be used in the question?

_____

_____

11. In a health class, the teacher wants students to consider the different ways that people can exercise during the winter, both indoors and outdoors. Which term should be used in the question?

_____

_____

12. In a geography class, the teacher wants students to show they know all of the types of bodies of water on the earth. Which term should be used in the question?

_____

_____

Point out to the students that the key words in an essay question are not only the essay test terms but also the *subjects of the questions*. They should be able to distinguish being asked to trace the events leading up to the Revolutionary War and the main events during the war, or between being asked to compare the works of a number of great American artists and compare the artists' lives. Students should cultivate the habit of taking the time to read questions carefully.

OUTLINING THE ANSWER

If an essay question calls for a long or complex answer, students should outline it before beginning to respond. The outline will help students organize their answers and include all the important concepts and facts. Because an outline gives order to the answer, it greatly facilitates the actual writing of it; turning the outline points into sentences is a simple matter.

When making an outline, students should think back to their notes. How was the material organized there? Also, which essay test terms are used in the question? What is its subject? It helps to visualize the notes, reading, and lectures about the topic. What points were covered? What was emphasized? The goal is to try to cover all the main concepts and facts that the teacher will be looking for when grading the question.

Point out the following facts about the use of outlines to your students:

- An outline should be brief, using short phrases and abbreviations and leaving out the little connecting words. Don't spend a lot of time writing your outline; its purpose is to ensure order and completeness to your answer. Don't try to formulate your sentences in the outline. Spend just a few minutes on it and leave the better part of the time allotted in your schedule to writing out the answer. (If you need to review how to make an outline, see Figure 3.3.)

- Keep all the key words in the exam question in mind so that your answer will fit the question. When you feel your outline is complete, look it over to make sure that it completely covers the important points and is logically organized. Be sure the information is in the order in which you will want it in the written-out answer. If you want to change the order of the main headings or subtopics, don't rewrite the entire outline. That will waste valuable time. Just renumber them.

- When you make your outline, include the relevant facts that you memorized and jotted down just before starting the test. Look them over to see if any of them apply to the answer you have outlined. Insert any that do into the appropriate spot in the outline. Don't rewrite them there, though. Just identify them in some way (perhaps with asterisks or circled letters or numbers) and put the symbol in the appropriate spot in the outline so when you are writing out your answer, you will know where to include the fact.

- You should write your outline on clean notebook paper separate from your answers or on the back pages of the exam booklet, if one is provided. If you run out of time before you have a chance to write out one of your answers, you can at least turn in the outline. Although you probably won't get full credit for the answer, you will get some points for showing that you know the important elements.

- If your time runs out and you must turn in an outline instead of an essay, be sure to indicate on the outline which question it is for and insert it in the proper order between the other essay answers. Then write a quick note at the top of the outline to let your instructor know that you ran out of time before you could put it in paragraph form. Ask the teacher to evaluate the outline as your answer to the question.

WRITING OUT THE ANSWER

A student's goal is to write a compact, complete, organized, and clear essay in answer to each question. Knowing a little and presenting it well is better than knowing a lot and presenting it poorly. A logical outline is a solid beginning.

The Opening Statement

Instruct the students to rephrase the question as an opening statement. This is the start to the answer. With an opening statement before them, their thoughts will be more likely to flow. Have them practice writing opening statements with Test Prep: Exercise 7.2. (A form for students to use to practice writing their own opening statements is provided in Appendix B.)

TEST PREP: EXERCISE 7.2

For each question below, pick out the essay test terms and the subjects, then rewrite the question as an opening statement. Students can refer to the notes for each question on the indicated pages.
Review the first question with students as an example. (Answers are in the back of the book in Appendix A.)

Example Question:

List the three branches of the U.S. government and identify what they include. (See notes in Figure 4.1.)

Exam Term(s):	list, identify
Subject of Question:	three branches of U.S. government
Opening Statement:	The three branches of the U.S. government are the executive, legislative, and judicial branches.

1. Question:

Identify three late-19th-century American authors and their works. (See notes in Test Prep: Exercise 4.1.)

Exam Term(s):	
Subject of Question:	
Opening Statement:	

---

2. Question:

   Describe the steps in the formation of RNA. (See notes in Figure 4.3.)

Exam Term(s):	
Subject of Question:	
Opening Statement:	

3. Question:

   Trace the events leading up to the Revolutionary War in America. (See notes in Figure 4.4.)

Exam Term(s):	
Subject of Question:	
Opening Statement:	

4. Question:

   Compare and contrast the great American art forms and works of Georgia O'Keeffe, Louis Tiffany, and Frank Lloyd Wright. (See notes in Test Prep: Exercise 4.3.)

Exam Term(s):	
Subject of Question:	
Opening Statement:	

5. Question:

   Discuss some of the effects of the Civil War in America. (See notes in Figure 4.7.)

Exam Term(s):	
Subject of Question:	
Opening Statement:	

6. Question:

   Discuss the differences and similarities between lines of latitude and lines of longitude. (See notes in Test Prep: Exercise 4.3.)

Exam Term(s):	
Subject of Question:	
Opening Statement:	

Essay Paragraphs

After they write the opening statement, have students refer to their outline and give the information in the first main heading, keeping key words of the question in mind. Then they should complete the paragraph with subtopics—two to four details, examples, or supporting information—and include relevant facts.

The second paragraph to give information should be started under the second main heading, and so on. When they have covered all the main headings in the outline, have them write one or two sentences to summarize their answer. A clear beginning and ending to the answer will make it seem well thought out.

The point that students should grasp is that this pattern is a *deductive* one, going from the main idea to the specifics. On being asked to give the details first and then arrive at the main idea, they would use *inductive* organization. In this case, they would work from the bottom of each main topic to the top—or from the specifics to the subtopics to the main idea.

As they write their answers, students should qualify specifics if they are unsure whether they remember them correctly. For example, it is better to say "toward the end of the 18th century" than "in 1793" if one is not sure whether it was 1793 or 1783. Often, an approximation is all that is necessary.

After finishing the essay, students should leave sufficient space for adding essential information that they might think of later.

Neatness

Any teacher will be favorably impressed by legible handwriting, ample margins, and separation of paragraphs by indentations. Research has shown that these elements of neatness are important variables in scoring. So in writing their answers, students should keep the following points in mind:

1. *Write your words so that they can be read* by others. If your handwriting is hard to read, you might try printing your answer.

2. *Try to use correct spelling, punctuation, and grammar.* Your teacher will be more impressed with your answer if you use traditional spelling and grammar and appropriate punctuation.

3. When you start a new idea or a new paragraph, *indent* to separate it from the previous paragraph. This is a way to show your teacher how many ideas or examples you have been able to recall and discuss.

4. *Leave sufficient margins* along all four sides of the page. This makes the answer look neater. It also allows room for you to insert additional information that you realize at the last minute you have left out.

5. *Erase or cross out carefully.* Don't leave your paper smudged and torn up from erasing. And don't make your teacher wonder what is and is not part of your answer. Make your changes clear and easy to follow.

RE-READING ANSWERS

Once they have completed the essays for each question, students ought to re-read them. When writing in haste, it is easy to misspell words, write illegibly, miswrite dates and figures, and omit words (or parts of words) and even parts of answers. As they go back over their essays, they should watch for these common errors, checking as well to see that they used all the memorized facts possible. For any lengthy additions, they can use the space they left after their answer and draw an arrow from the information to the part of the answer where it applies. These last-minute corrections and additions may add appreciably to their grades and generally improve the impressions their papers will make on the teacher. But they should be sure to make them as neat as possible.

MAKING A FINAL CHECK

Instruct your students to make a final check in the last few minutes before the testing session ends. They should make sure their name and any other necessary information (date, class name, section number) is on every page of their answers. Then they should gather their answers together and check the order of the pages. When turning in the test, they should ask the teacher if they also need to turn in their scratch paper containing the outlines and jotted-down facts. If so, students should indicate at the top of each page that it is a "scratch sheet."

CHAPTER SUMMARY

To take an essay test, students need to budget their time after assessing the number of questions and choosing the ones that seem the easiest to answer. Students will need to allow time to read the questions carefully, paying attention to the essay test terms and the subjects of the questions. Then, if the question calls for a long-answer essay, they should outline the answer so it will include all the important points from study notes and the list of memorized facts jotted down just before starting the test.

In writing their answer from the outline, students should keep the following pattern in mind:

1. Write an *opening statement* that rephrases the question.

2. Develop the *main points* of the outline one paragraph at a time.

3. Follow the topic sentence (main point) of each paragraph with two to four *details, examples, or supportive citations*.

4. Write a *one- or two-sentence summary*.

5. Leave *room between each answer* to add more information if needed after re-reading it.

Finally, students should try to give themselves enough time to re-read their answers and make a final check. Should they run out of time before writing one of the essays, they can at least hand in the outline.

8

Taking the Objective Test

Having completed the steps listed in Chapter 6 for organizing themselves to take the test, students are ready to begin. Their best insurance that they will do well will be having studied the subject thoroughly (as described in Chapters 3 and 5). There are some special techniques for taking objective tests, however, that students must know.

First, they need to have a strategy for taking the test; turning the test in after going through it once is not really enough. This chapter will cover learning how to pace themselves so they'll have time to go through the test a second time and then make a final check before they turn it in.

Then they'll learn how to look for cues in the questions that will help them recognize the right answer. Some kinds of cues apply to several kinds of objective questions; other cues are specific to multiple-choice, matching, true/false, or completion questions. Finally, they'll learn when and how to guess on questions they cannot answer from their knowledge and their search for cues.

TEST-TAKING STEPS

To give themselves the chance to answer correctly all the questions they can, they need to budget their time (as pointed out in Chapter 6). For an objective test, they'll want enough time to go through it three times. First, they should go through and answer all the questions they know, spending an equal amount of time on each one and not getting bogged down on difficult questions. (If some test sections are worth more than others, however, more time should be allowed for those. If it isn't possible to tell how many points the sections or questions are worth, students should ask the teacher immediately.)

The second time through the test, the goal is to try to answer the questions they couldn't the first time. (Some cues will be provided later in this chapter to help identify the right answer.) The third time through, their focus should be on going back over their entire answer sheet and checking for forgotten questions, stray marks, and misnumbered answers.

Budgeting Time

To figure out how to budget time for a test, students first need to know the total length of the test session. Have them subtract five minutes for reading all the directions thoroughly and decide on a test-taking schedule, and have them subtract another five minutes for their final check. So if they have 55 minutes to take a test, they will subtract 10 from 55, leaving 45 minutes for the first and second go-throughs.

To decide how much time they can spend on each question, students need to know how many questions are on the test and then allot a little more time for the first go-through than for the second. For example, on a test having 50 objective questions worth two points each, students could spend half a minute on each question the first time through, for a total of 25 minutes. This would leave 20 minutes for the second go-through. A diagram of that test-taking schedule would look like the one in Figure 8.1.

Reading the Directions

Students should be instructed to read all the directions carefully before they start to answer any questions. If there are directions for each section of the test, they should re-read these before beginning to answer any questions in the section.

It is important they should read the directions critically and not assume they already know what they say. For example, on a multiple-choice test, it is easy to assume that one is to select the best answer. The directions, however, might tell you to select the least appropriate answer. Or one might assume that for true/false questions, one is to indicate T or

Figure 8.1

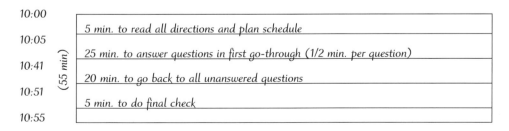

F. But the directions might tell the student to answer yes or no or to change all false statements to make them true. Or one might assume that for matching questions, the object is to match the Column 2 items to the Column 1 items by writing the letter or number from Column 2 next to its match in Column 1, when the directions really indicate drawing a line from each item in Column 1 to its match in Column 2. In short, by ignoring the directions, test takers might not get proper credit for their answers, even if they know the material thoroughly.

The First Go-Through

Having read the directions carefully and planned a schedule for taking the test, the students are ready to begin answering questions. On this first go-through, they will answer the questions that are easy for them. Remind your students, however, that they should read all the choices for each question before answering, even if they think they have spotted the right answer. (Taking an objective test in pencil is strongly recommended!) They should keep in mind the following points as they work their way through the test the first time:

- *Attempt every question but answer only the easiest ones the first time through.* Remember, questions that look difficult and involved may turn out not to be. Work through the entire test, item by item, no matter how hard some of the items may appear. Spend your allotted time on each question.
- *Read each question thoroughly and critically.* The difference between a right and a wrong answer can often be a single word.
- *Don't overinterpret questions.* The more time you spend laboring over a question—once you have read it carefully—the more likely you are to read something into it that's not there. Students sometimes think that the right answer is too obvious and that the teacher must be trying to trick them. Most teachers don't do this. The right answer may seem obvious simply because you know the material well.
- *Establish a system for going back to questions later.* This will help you with your second go-through. If you answer a question and then feel a little unsure about it, put a small pencil dot next to it. On a multiple-choice test, you might have narrowed down the answer to a couple of alternatives, so mark them with a light pencil check. Then you can save time during the second go-through by ignoring the alternatives you're sure are wrong. For matching questions, you might lightly check the items still to be matched. For true/false and completion questions, you might lightly check the ones you think you have an answer for (there might be cues in later questions that could confirm the answer) and place a small dot next to those you have no idea about. Whatever the symbols, it is important to make some "signposts" for the second go-through.

The Second Go-Through

As soon as students get through the last item on the test, they are ready to begin their second go-through. If they have been following a preset schedule, they should have time to go back to all the unanswered questions, starting with those at the beginning of the test.

Students should understand that they need not be concerned if other students finish the test ahead of them. The latter might be finishing faster because they know the material better, but it is just as likely they have finished early because they do not know the answers to many of the questions. Comparing themselves to these other students will only make them unnecessarily anxious and waste their time!

On the second go-through, students should first go back to those questions they've checked—the ones for which they've narrowed down alternatives or have some idea of what the right answer might be. These are the questions that will be easiest to answer, so it is desirable to have time to do so. Then, if there's still time, they can go back to those questions with a small dot—the ones that seem extremely difficult. The goal in this second go-through is to answer as many questions on the test as possible.

Here are some tips to give students to help them decide on the best answer to questions about which they feel unsure:

- *Read section and question directions again.* Make sure that your difficulty with the question is not due to misreading the directions or the question.
- *If the question seems particularly complicated, underline key words.* Sometimes emphasizing key words will help clarify the main idea of the question.
- *Put difficult questions into your own words.* Sometimes rephrasing a question can make it clear. But be careful not to change the meaning.
- *If a question is not clear in spite of all your efforts to understand it, ask your teacher.* It is possible that a word might be missing or that there is a typographical error. You can't ask the teacher for clarification of standardized tests, however, because the teacher must keep everything "standard" and cannot give special help or information to just one student.
- *Reason through each question.* An acceptable alternative can be selected by a process of reasoning, knowledge, and elimination. For example, in multiple-choice or matching questions, balance the alternatives against each other; the differences may help you judge which is the best answer.
- *Eliminate wrong answer options.* Recognize that what you know to be incorrect is as valuable as what you know to be correct. Lightly cross out or eliminate answers that are wrong. This will help you focus on the possible correct answers.
- *Try to recall your class lectures.* It is sometimes helpful to try to recall what your teacher said about the subject of a question that seems particularly difficult. Based on how your teacher presented the subject in class, try to figure out which answer he or she intended to be right.

- *Look for cues, or clues, to help you answer the question.* Later in this chapter is information about different kinds of cues, which include grammatical agreement, synonyms, qualifying and absolute words, position of alternatives, and inter-item cues.

- *Don't be afraid to change an answer* if, after going through the test the first time, you have reason to believe your first answer is wrong. Research shows that students who change their original answer choices because of careful reconsideration and discovering inter-item cues do increase their test scores. The key to changing answers successfully, however, is the ability to recognize the difference between selecting a different answer for a good reason and just being uncertain about the right answer. Some students are better at recognizing this difference than others. To assess your ability to change answers for the better, save a few tests and compare the number of times you changed a wrong answer to a right one with the number of times you changed a right one to a wrong one.

Final Check

After having worked so hard to prepare for this test, students should be willing to spend the last five minutes before turning it in making sure that there are no careless errors. Students should be instructed that their final check should include the following steps:

1. *Go back to any answers you meant to change and make sure you made those changes on the answer sheet.* Be sure to erase the original answer completely, especially if you have a machine-scorable answer sheet.

2. *Spot-check your answer sheet to be sure you put down the answers you intended.* If you left some answers blank the first time through, be sure you didn't inadvertently fill them in with answers to subsequent questions. If your answers were hastily written, fix any that might be misinterpreted by the person correcting the test.

3. *If there is no penalty for guessing, use the appropriate guessing strategy* of those described at the end of this chapter to fill in any blanks on the answer sheet. *If there is a penalty for guessing, do not guess;* instead, try to find the question in the test. It is possible that you already worked out the answer but did not record it on the answer sheet.

4. *Quickly check for stray marks and erase them,* especially if you are using a machine-scorable answer sheet. Stray marks can be picked up by the test-scoring machine and counted as errors.

5. *Erase any dots, checks, and underlining on the test* (unless you were allowed to write your answers on the test). It is possible that other students will be using the same test, so you should return it in the same condition in which you received it. This is why your checks, dots, and underlining should be written in pencil, very lightly.

6. *Be sure your name and other necessary information is on every page of your test* (if your answers are marked on the test) or answer sheet. If you

used scratch paper to work out problems or jot down formulas or other information from memory, put your name on that, too, and label it "scratch sheet." Gather all these test materials and turn them in.

TEST QUESTION CUES

Although no substitute for thorough study, knowing how to find cues (clues) to the answers in objective questions is an important skill. Some cues can be found in all (or several) kinds of objective tests. These cues, which are explained in the following sections, are as follows:

- Inter-item cues
- Qualifying and absolute words
- Grammatical agreement
- Word associations and synonyms

Other cues (length, position, and generality of multiple-choice alternatives, for example) are specific to particular kinds of objective tests and will be explained in the sections about each of the four kinds of objective questions.

Cues are more often found in teacher-made than in standardized tests. The publishers of standardized tests have huge staffs of test experts and spend a great deal of time and money to avoid flaws in their tests. Teachers, however, may not be experts in making test questions and do not have unlimited time or assistance to develop their tests. Consequently, most of the cues described in this chapter apply only to teacher-made tests.

A word of caution about cues: Students should not spend too much time searching for them. They should use their knowledge of the material to answer questions and look for cues only if they are uncertain about the right answers.

Inter-Item Cues

Students should understand that one question in a test may provide information about the answer to another; this is an inter-item cue. It is difficult for a teacher to write a long objective exam covering a limited number of topics without having information in some questions relate to other questions. When the student is unsure of an answer to a question, the strategy of choice is to come back to it the second time through. The student may find information in another question that suggests the answer or helps to eliminate one or more alternatives. Conversely, the student may also find information while working through the test that suggests a reason to change a previous answer.

Inter-item cues are very important and very reliable. These are informational cues and can definitely help the student get a better score. The other cues that will be discussed are probability cues, which can only increase one's chances of answering a question correctly.

The two sets of test questions shown in Figure 8.2 can be used to provide students with examples of inter-item cues. Even though it can take extra time and thought, using these cues may help students figure out some answers.

Figure 8.2

Example 1

   1. The orthograde skeletal structure of *Homo sapiens* is most similar to that of which of the following:
      A. Beavers
      B. Apes
      C. Bears
      D. Deer

   37. An animal with an orthograde skeletal structure is said to
      A. live in water.
      B. walk on two legs.
      C. walk on four legs.
      D. have no foramen magnum.

   The first question tells you that *Homo sapiens* has an orthograde skeletal structure. Therefore, when you come to question 37, you can infer that B must be the correct answer. And by selecting the correct answer to question 37, you could then infer that B is the correct answer to question 1, because the only alternative that walks on two legs is apes.

Example 2

   1. Which of the following foods would count toward the five servings of grains that the food pyramid requires you eat each day?
      A. Pasta
      B. Ice cream
      C. Chocolate
      D. Apples

   45. It is important to eat _____ servings of grains, such as spaghetti, per day.
      A. 6
      B. 20
      C. 5
      D. 1

   Question 1 has already told you that you need five servings of grains per day. Therefore, when you come to question 45, you know that the correct answer is C. By the same token, reading question 45 carefully, you can readily infer that spaghetti is a type of pasta (the obvious choice for question 1), confirming that the correct answer to question 1 must therefore be A.

Inter-item cues can be used with matching questions to help make matches one was uncertain of during the first go-through. They can also provide a clue as to whether a statement is true or false as well as the answer to a completion question.

Qualifying and Absolute Words

Another skill used by well-prepared test takers is to be alert to the use of qualifiers. An alternative or a statement that contains a qualifying word—such as *generally, often, some,* or *most*—is more likely to be correct than one that contains an absolute word—such as *always, never, all,* or *nobody.* This is because very few things are absolute, and it takes only one exception to make an absolute statement false or incorrect.

For example, invite students to compare the following true/false questions:

1. All students know how to take tests. True or False

2. Some students know how to take tests. True or False

The word *all* in statement 1 makes the statement false because it is too inclusive. The word *some* in statement 2 makes the statement true; it acknowledges that there are some students who know how to take tests and some who do not.

The lists below contain absolute words, which usually indicate a false statement or an incorrect alternative, and qualifying words, which usually indicate a true statement or a correct alternative.

ABSOLUTE WORDS

always	everything	completely
never	everyone	exactly
necessarily	only	exclusively
definitely	no	cannot
must	without exception	no matter what
all	everybody	nobody
none	no one	
impossible	every	

QUALIFYING WORDS

generally	may	sometimes
usually	maybe	occasionally
some	most	often
frequently	on the average	perhaps
seldom	rarely	probably

Students should not rely entirely on absolute and qualifying words to judge a statement or alternative, however. An experienced test maker can write a false statement without using an absolute word. Or a theorem, law, or rule to which there is no exception can be presented with an absolute word and still be a true statement or correct alternative; for example, "E always equals mc^2."

Sometimes there is no absolute or a qualifying word in a statement or alternative, but it is stated in such a specific or absolute way that it implies there are no exceptions. These statements should be handled in the same way as statements with absolute words. Unless there truly can never be an exception, they should be treated as false or incorrect.

Have students consider the following multiple-choice question as an example:

1. When taking an objective test, it is a good idea to
   A. never guess an answer.
   B. generally guess if you don't know the answer.
   C. cheat.
   D. usually expect to do very poorly.

Alternative C does not contain an absolute word, but always is implied. Therefore, you would reject C, just as you would reject A, which contains the absolute word *never*. That narrows your choices to B and D—and common sense (and having studied this book) tells you that D is incorrect.

Grammatical Agreement

Yet another hint students can learn to look for is instances where one can eliminate a choice that does not agree grammatically with the stem of a multiple-choice or matching question or with the sentence structure of a completion question. Sometimes the verb tenses or pronoun references do not agree. It may not be possible to define the grammatical error, but it will be obvious that somehow the choice does not sound right. Of course, typing errors do happen. If the student feels fairly certain that an alternative is the right one, even though it is not in grammatical agreement, it is probably better to pick it anyway.

Use of A *and* An. The article *a* is used with words that begin with consonants, and the article *an* is used with words that begin with vowels. Although a careful test writer would put an article with each alternative instead of in the stem, students might occasionally encounter a question such as the following:

1. A biologist who specializes in the study of the relationships of an organism to its environment is known as an
   A. ecologist.
   B. structuralist.
   C. taxonomist.
   D. naturalist.

Because the stem ends with the article *an*, the correct alternative must be A—ecologist—the only one that begins with a vowel.

Singular and Plural Verbs and Nouns. Multiple-choice and completion questions both require completing a sentence. The student's choice should make a grammatically correct sentence. So if the stem of a multiple-choice question uses a plural verb, the correct alternative will contain a plural noun or object; if the stem uses a singular verb, the alternative should also be singular. For example, if the alternatives to a stem that used *are* were (A) bone, (B) ear, (C) muscle, and (D) nerves, the obvious choice would be D, the only plural noun.

For a matching question, using the singular-plural cue is also appropriate. A plural lead in Column 1 should match a plural alternative in Column 2, and a singular lead should match a singular alternative. Look at the following example:

1. children	A. infants
2. female	B. boy and girl
3. male	C. woman
4. families	D. man
5. babies	E. mothers and their children

The only likely matches to 1, 4, and 5 are A, B, and E because they are plural. Similarly, the only probable matches to 2 and 3 are C and D, the only singular choices. So even if you did not know the answers to this matching question, you could at least narrow down the choices by using the singular-plural cue.

Word Associations and Synonyms

In multiple-choice and matching questions, student may find that a word in the stem has a direct relationship to a word in one of the alternatives. The following multiple-choice question illustrates such a synonym cue:

The *Strong Vocational Interest Blank* is used to measure

A. aptitudes.
B. likes and dislikes.
C. achievement.
D. adjustment.

The word *interest* in the stem is synonymous with *likes and dislikes*, or alternative B. Of course, in some questions, the synonym is not the correct choice. The student should give precedence to choosing the correct answer over using this cue.

Word-association cues are sometimes less obvious than synonyms, but they can be identified by carefully reading the alternatives. The following multiple-choice question is an example of a word-association cue:

1. Charles Dickens's *Hard Times* is about the
   A. difficult life of a factory worker.
   B. politics of the French château country.
   C. court of King Edward III.
   D. limitations of European existentialism.

It will be noticed that the book's title is *Hard Times*. The phrase *difficult life* in alternative A has about the same meaning. So one could make an educated guess by using this cue, without necessarily having read the book.

ANSWERING MULTIPLE-CHOICE QUESTIONS

Students should grasp that their task is to read the stem, select the best possible alternative, and mark that answer. Selecting the best alternative is the hardest part of that task, but several techniques can make it easier.

Anticipating the Answer

Multiple-choice tests can be difficult when all the alternatives, or "foils," seem true. The instructions, however, usually tell the student to select the *best* alternative. That is why a good strategy is to read the stem and then anticipate the answer before reading the alternatives. After anticipating the answer, the student can look for it among the alternatives offered.

Even though students may not anticipate the exact answer, they will probably anticipate some major component of the answer. Therefore, as they read the alternatives, they can narrow the choices to those that contain that major component. One note of caution: Students should read and consider all the alternatives, even if they first spot one that contains the major component they anticipated. It is possible that more than one alternative will contain the component, and the point is to select the best one.

If the anticipated component is not in any of the alternatives, then choosing the best answer becomes a matter of focusing on the choices offered, determining how well each of them answers the question, and selecting the one that makes the most sense.

Eliminating Unlikely Alternatives

The key to taking a multiple-choice test is the ability to eliminate answers or narrow down the possibilities. This increases the odds of getting the correct answer, whether or not the student feels sure of the material.

Eliminating alternatives necessitates the application of one's reasoning abilities. If the student is asked to choose the correct theorem to be used for a geometry problem, and one of the alternatives is evidently not a theorem, reason dictates that alternative should be eliminated.

When several alternatives seem correct, or if none of them does, comparing them to see how they are alike or different is a next-best option. By balancing the alternatives against one another, students should be able to eliminate one or two based on what they know about the topic.

One way to eliminate alternatives is to treat each as if it were a true-false statement. Lightly mark in pencil a T or an F by the alternative after you have read it with the stem.

Using Cues

In the preceding section, we looked at cues, or clues, that are applicable to all or most kinds of objective questions—inter-item cues, qualifying and absolute words, grammatical agreement, and word association and synonyms. Besides these, several other cues are specific to multiple-choice questions. These cues can be found in the alternatives.

The Most General Alternative. The correct alternative is often the most general, because the most general alternative often is the most-encompassing choice. The student will often find a list with technical and specific alternatives along with one that is more general. Chances are good that the general one is the correct answer. The following two questions are examples:

1. The lungs
   A. are solid and immobile and located within the chest.
   B. are the only organs that produce insulin.
   C. function primarily in respiration.
   D. possess the sphincter of Oddi.

Even without being sure of the correct answer, one can see that the alternatives A, B, and D all deal with specific facts and details about the lungs. Alternative C deals with a main feature of the lungs—respiration. Because C is the more general answer and allows for more variability, it is logically the best one.

1. In geometry, an angle
   A. is always between 90 and 180 degrees.
   B. is always 90 degrees.
   C. is a small circle.
   D. consists of two lines.

Even without being certain of the correct answer, the student can see that the alternatives A, B, and C deal with specific geometric facts or shapes. D deals with a main feature of angles, the fact that they consist of two lines. Because D is the most general answer and allows for more variability, it is logically the best one.

Two Similar Alternatives. If two alternatives have nearly the same meaning, then both are probably not correct—unless a key word or phrase is different. Following are examples of questions with two alternatives that mean essentially the same thing:

1. The Treaty of Brest Litovsk was ratified by Moscow because
    A. Tsar Alexander I wanted to prevent Napoleon's invasion of Russia.
    B. Austria was outproducing Russia in armaments.
    C. Russia could not keep pace with the military production of its enemies.
    D. Lenin wanted to get the Soviet Union out of World War I.

Because alternatives B and C have very similar meanings, the student should choose the answer from alternatives A or D. If two alternatives mean the same thing and only one correct answer is being asked for, the best move is to eliminate the two similar answers.

1. Seashores experience a change in water level every day called a tide. Tides are caused by which of the following:
    A. The slant of the beach
    B. The gravitational pull of the moon
    C. The shape of the beach
    D. Ships at sea

Because alternatives A and C have very similar meanings, the student ought to choose the answer from alternatives B and D. Again, if two alternatives mean the same thing, and only one correct answer is being asked for, the two similar answers should be eliminated.

Alternatives With Opposite Meanings. If two alternatives have opposite meanings, one of them is more likely to be the correct answer, because when answer options for a question are being developed, an antonym for the correct answer is often a logical alternative to include. Following are two examples of questions with two alternatives with opposite meaning:

1. The planarian has
    A. an anterior brain.
    B. three legs.
    C. red eyes.
    D. a posterior brain.

Alternatives A and D are opposites, so alternatives B and C can be eliminated, unless the student knows one of them is the correct answer. Because alternatives A and D have opposite meanings, one of them is probably the correct answer.

1. Polar bears can live in the icy Arctic because
    A. they build fires.
    B. they have thick white fur and layers of fat.
    C. they have no fur.
    D. they huddle close together.

Alternatives B and C are opposites, so one of them is probably the correct answer. Alternatives A and D can be eliminated right away, unless the student is sure one of them is the correct answer.

None or All-of-the-Above Alternatives. If one of the alternatives in a multiple-choice question is "none of the above" or "all of the above," the best approach is for the student to read the stem and then subject each alternative to a true/false test, lightly penciling a T or an F next to each alternative. Upon reaching the alternative that says "none of the above" or "all of the above," the student need only look back at the results for the other alternatives. An F by all of them indicates that "none of the above" is probably the correct answer. A T by all of them, alternatively, indicates the answer is probably "all of the above."

Having marked some T and some F, however, allows the student to eliminate "all of the above" or "none of the above" and pick the answer from the alternatives marked T. If there are four alternatives and one of them is "none of the above," while two are marked F, and the fourth one is uncertain, the student's answer will either be "none of the above" or the fourth alternative.

A variation of the none or all-of-the-above alternative is an answer choice indicating that two out of three (or three out of four) alternatives are correct; for example, "B and C above." If the student marked alternatives B and C with a T, then that alternative is correct. If the student marked one T and one F, however, then "B and C above" is not correct and should be eliminated.

The Middle Value. When the alternatives are numerical values or a range (from old to new, early to late, small to big, for example) and you are not sure which one is correct, the extremes can usually be eliminated, as demonstrated by the following multiple-choice example:

1. The mature human has how many teeth?
   A. 15
   B. 32
   C. 54
   D. 7

In the event of being unsure of the answer, the student's wisest choice would be to eliminate the two extremes, C and D, then choose from the remaining answers. (In this case, one could simply use the information available in one's head—counting one's teeth and choosing B!)

The Length of Alternatives. Many tests are fairly consistent about the length of correct answers. If most of the correct answers have been the shortest alternatives and the student has no informational cues, picking the shortest of the possible alternatives arguably has the greatest likelihood of success. Conversely, if most of the correct answers have been the longest alternatives, it would be best to pick the longest of the alternatives that have not been eliminated.

Failing a noticeable tendency for the correct answers to be the longest or the shortest, the best choice may be the longest alternative—if it is the most inclusive of the choices and does not contain or imply an absolute word.

The Position of Alternatives. A caveat: This is one of the weakest cues and should be used by the student only after having searched fruitlessly for all other cues. One cannot know if the teacher has made a conscious effort to avoid always using the same position for the correct answers. Additionally, on professionally constructed (i.e., standardized) tests, the test makers would know to avoid this particular cue.

The student skims the answer sheet to see if most of the correct answers are in the same position. If there is a pattern and the student has no other basis for selecting an alternative, then choosing the answer in that position is the likeliest guess. Sometimes one of the middle alternatives, especially if it has the most words, is slightly more often correct. Research has shown that in four-item multiple-choice questions, B and C are the correct answers slightly more often than the other alternatives. (This is because some teachers, who are inexperienced with test construction, tend to decide that the first and last choices, A and D, look too obvious.)

ANSWERING MATCHING QUESTIONS

Reading the directions carefully before answering a matching question is always advisable. There may be extra alternatives in Column 2 compared with the number of stems in Column 1, or more than one alternative might match with each stem, or test directions may indicate drawing lines to connect the matches, or the student may have to write the letters identifying the alternatives beside their match in Column 1. If the directions are not clear, one should ask the teacher.

The recommended procedure is for the student to read through both columns to get a sense of all the choices. Even though initially some of them seem to be good matches, it is possible that more than one alternative could fit.

Instruct your students to follow these steps when working through a matching question:

1. *On the first go-through, make all the matches you are sure of.* Check off the alternatives in Column 2 as you use them (unless the directions tell you that each alternative can be used more than once). The key to answering matching questions is the same as that to answering multiple-choice questions: eliminate as many possibilities as you can.

2. *Leave the alternatives you are not sure of* and work your way through the rest of the test. Come back to those questions when you find inter-item cues that can help.

3. *On your second go-through, come back to the unfinished matching questions and look for cues,* including those of grammatical agreement and word association discussed earlier in this chapter, and the cues specific to matching questions, which will be discussed next.

Matching-Question Cues

Students can look for two special kinds of cues in matching questions to help them narrow their choices—a mixture of categories and the position of the alternatives in Column 2.

Mixture of Categories. In a matching question on a history test, for example, one might find names, dates, and events. In the first column, there may be stems of events and names to match with dates and events in the second column. Because it is improbable that one would match an event with an event or a date with a name, it is possible to narrow one's choices.

In the example below, names in Column 1 probably match events in Column 2, and the events in Column 1 should probably match dates in Column 2. Have students figure out the likely matches for the stems in Column 1.

Column 1	*Column 2*
1. Event	A. Date
2. Name	B. Event
3. Event	C. Date
4. Name	D. Event
5. Event	E. Date
6. Name	F. Event

Instead of having six possible matches for each stem, we find only three. While three possible answers are still a lot, the probability of guessing correctly has increased, and a good knowledge of the material should help the student narrow down the matches even further. For stems 1, 3, and 5 in Column 1, a student would select a match from alternatives A, C, and E in Column 2. For stems 2, 4, and 6 the student would consider alternatives B, D, and F.

Position Cues. If a student cannot decide between two or three matches, one cue that will help select the best match is the position of the alternatives. The teacher has probably tried not to put the matching alternative in Column 2 directly across from its stem in Column 1. So if one of the possible matches is across from the stem, it is ordinarily safe for the student to assume it is not the correct one.

The teacher will often decide at the last minute to add one or two extra alternatives to Column 2 to make the question more challenging. These extras will probably be at the bottom of the column because the teacher didn't have time to retype the entire question. Because students don't know if their teacher was in a hurry, this is not a reliable cue. They should use it only after having made all the matches they can based on their knowledge of the material and eliminating all the alternatives they can by using other cues. If it comes down to a choice between an alternative in the middle of the list and one at the bottom, the middle alternative would be the likelier option.

The matching question in Figure 8.3 illustrates how to use position cues.

Figure 8.3

Directions: Write the letter of the correct answer from Column 2 in the answer blank next to Column 1. Use each answer only once.

Answers *Column 1*   *Column 2*

   C   1. anthropologist   ✓   A. community and family life

   D   2. astronomer   ✓   B. meanings and psychological effects of words

          3. geologist   ✓   C. human development

   H   4. biologist   ✓   D. celestial phenomena

   J   5. botanist   E. language

   I   6. zoologist   F. insect forms

          7. entomologist   G. the earth

          8. philologist   ✓   H. all forms of living matter

   B   9. semanticist   ✓   I. animal life

   A   10. sociologist   ✓   J. plant life

                                                   K. problems of aging

                                                 L. mental disease

---

Let us suppose that the test taker has used all available knowledge and other cues to make the matches shown in the answer column and has checked off the matched alternatives in Column 2. But the student has no idea of the answers to stems 3, 7, and 8 with five alternatives left in Column 2. Through use of the same-line position cue, G can probably be eliminated as a match for 7.

With use of the end-of-the-column position cue, K and L can probably be eliminated entirely. The answer to 7 is therefore most likely E or F. If the test taker picks F (the correct match), that leaves alternatives E and C to match with stems 3 and 8. Students can use their knowledge and reasoning ability to choose, or if that isn't any help, they can simply guess (and have a 50–50 chance of being correct). If the test taker in this example guessed correctly, G would be matched with 3 and E with 8.

ANSWERING TRUE/FALSE QUESTIONS

True/false questions test not only our knowledge of the material but also our ability to do careful and critical reading. We must pay attention to every word in a true/false statement yet guard against reading information into it that isn't there as well as against trying too hard to find exceptions to every statement. To illustrate the problem with overinterpreting, have students read the following statement:

    1. Psychology is the science that studies why human beings behave as they do.
       True or **False?**

It might be tempting for students to say that this statement is false because they remember from their notes that psychology also studies animal behavior. The prepared student realizes, however, that just because this statement does not contain an exhaustive definition of psychology, it should not be judged false. If the statement had been worded "Psychology studies only human behavior," however, then it should have been marked false—the word *only* incorrectly limits the statement.

The hardest kind of true/false question is the mixed statement—in other words, one part is true and the other part is false. It bears reminding that unless the entire statement is true, the student should mark it false. A true/false test can also be made more challenging by asking the student to underline the elements that make statements false or to revise false statements to make them true. It cannot be stressed enough that students should always be sure to read test directions with care.

A sometimes overlooked survival skill when answering a series of true/false questions is to avoid getting bogged down on any one of them. Keeping up one's speed, allotting only the time scheduled for each question in the first go-through, can make a significant difference for the student. Questions one is not sure of should be left for the second go-through. Looking for inter-item cues can be sometimes prove quite helpful as the student continues through the test, as can using the cues of qualifying and absolute words discussed earlier in this chapter when the student comes back to questions that had to be skipped over.

Unlike in multiple-choice tests, the pattern of answers is not a cue in true/false tests. It does not matter if there is a long series of trues or falses or whether there are many more trues than falses, or vice versa.

ANSWERING COMPLETION QUESTIONS

Completion, or fill-in-the-blank, questions are the most difficult kind of objective questions because they force the student to recall the right answer rather than recognizing it among a number of alternatives. As with the other kinds of objective questions, however, it is important to read the directions and the questions very carefully.

Some of the cues that apply to the other objective questions are useful in helping students answer completion questions, too. They might, for example, look for cues of grammatical agreement. Is the word before the blank *a* or *an*? That furnishes a clue as to whether the missing word starts with a vowel or a consonant. Are the verbs, nouns, or pronouns that refer to the missing word singular or plural?

Here's another tip students should keep in mind: After filling in an answer, they should read the completed sentence quietly to themselves. Does it sound right? Sometimes hearing the sentence can stimulate their memory and help them decide if the choice they made was the right one.

Of course, inter-item cues are the most helpful. As with other kinds of objective tests, students should skip the questions they're not sure of the first time through. They may discover an answer in another question.

The length of the line to be filled in can sometimes be a cue, but it is not very reliable. Someone besides the teacher may have prepared the test and not known the intended answers. Or your teacher might have made all the blanks uniform to avoid this kind of cue or simply have made blanks that fit the available space.

Students should be aware that the answer may be more than one word; it could be a phrase or a sentence. If the directions do not indicate which, asking the teacher before the test is advisable. In cases where the student is uncertain of the exact word the teacher is looking for, writing in the word or phrase that comes to mind may at least receive partial credit for having the general idea.

WHEN AND HOW TO GUESS

It can happen that a student will have just about run out of time and yet still not have finished the test, despite his or her best efforts. In such cases—for some tests—guessing is a last-ditch option. It pays to know whether there will be a penalty for guessing, however. If this is not indicated in the test directions, the student should ask the teacher before starting to take the test. (Asking in the last three minutes of the test would be a dead giveaway!)

On most teacher-made tests, departmental tests, and standardized tests, there is no penalty for guessing. This means that student scores are based only on the number of correct answers; there are no penalties for incorrect answers. Answering every item on the test, whether one knows the answer or not, should be a student's goal.

On some standardized tests, however, there is a penalty for guessing. This usually means that one point (or however many points the question is worth) is subtracted for each unanswered question, but a fraction more than the value of the question is subtracted for each incorrect answer. The purpose of this penalty is to discourage students from wild guessing.

The amount of the penalty should determine how much students ought to guess. If the penalty is only one-fourth more than the value of the question, for example, and they can eliminate (by their knowledge or by cues in the test) at least one of the alternatives, they should go ahead and guess. If the penalty is greater—say, one-and-a-half times the value of the question—they should guess only if they have narrowed the possible alternatives to two.

If the exam is almost over and 15 or 20 percent of the questions remain unanswered (which can easily happen on a standardized or long test), students might use the last minute to do some wild guessing and answer every question—if there is no penalty for guessing. Because students may not want the person scoring the test to know they were guessing, it is better to mark a random variety of answer positions rather than mark all their guesses in the same column. Note that most standardized tests are scored by machines, which will not care whether the student was guessing or not.

Have students try the guessing experiments in Test Prep: Exercises 8.1 and 8.2 to see how many points they could pick up by randomly guessing on a true/false test and on a four-alternative multiple-choice test. (Answers can

---

TEST PREP: EXERCISE 8.1

Experimental True/False Test

Directions: Write a T or an F beside each number. Compare your answers with those in Appendix A. Each "correct" response counts as two points. Your score is based on the number of correct answers.

1. _____	11. _____	21. _____	31. _____	41. _____
2. _____	12. _____	22. _____	32. _____	42. _____
3. _____	13. _____	23. _____	33. _____	43. _____
4. _____	14. _____	24. _____	34. _____	44. _____
5. _____	15. _____	25. _____	35. _____	45. _____
6. _____	16. _____	26. _____	36. _____	46. _____
7. _____	17. _____	27. _____	37. _____	47. _____
8. _____	18. _____	28. _____	38. _____	48. _____
9. _____	19. _____	29. _____	39. _____	49. _____
10. _____	20. _____	30. _____	40. _____	50. _____

Your Wild Guessing Score _____

TEST PREP: EXERCISE 8.2

Experimental Multiple-Choice Test

Directions: Write A, B, C, or D beside each number. Compare your answers with those in Appendix A. Each "correct" response counts as two points. Your score is based on the number of correct answers.

1. _____	11. _____	21. _____	31. _____	41. _____
2. _____	12. _____	22. _____	32. _____	42. _____
3. _____	13. _____	23. _____	33. _____	43. _____
4. _____	14. _____	24. _____	34. _____	44. _____
5. _____	15. _____	25. _____	35. _____	45. _____
6. _____	16. _____	26. _____	36. _____	46. _____
7. _____	17. _____	27. _____	37. _____	47. _____
8. _____	18. _____	28. _____	38. _____	48. _____
9. _____	19. _____	29. _____	39. _____	49. _____
10. _____	20. _____	30. _____	40. _____	50. _____

Your Wild Guessing Score _____

be found in the back of the book in Appendix A.) They may give themselves 2 points for each question answered correctly; if all answers are correct, their score is 100 points for each test.

The purpose of the two experiments in Test Prep: Exercises 8.1 and 8.2 is not to show students that there's some chance they could pass an objective test without studying, there is no substitute for studying. The purpose is only to demonstrate that on tests in which there is no penalty for guessing, students could probably add a few points to their scores by randomly answering questions they do not have time to finish.

Many students feel timid about guessing. They may know that they can increase their score by guessing but refuse to do so because they believe it is unfair or dishonest to guess. But some standardized tests and many departmental and teacher-made tests are graded on a curve. This means that the highest scorers will get the As or get admitted to a college or a special program, while the lower scorers will get the lower grades and will not be admitted. Students who are willing to guess as a last resort will get higher scores than their peers who know just as much about the subject of the test but are not willing to guess.

There is another benefit to guessing. Not answering a question signals the teacher that a student knows nothing about that question. But chances are that student does have some idea about it and has perhaps even narrowed the alternatives. By guessing one of the remaining alternatives, a student has a chance to get credit for what she knows.

The best guarantee of a good grade, in summary, is thorough study. But students can add points to their score by guessing the answer after eliminating obviously wrong alternatives. This is really "educated guessing"— the guessing that is done after the choices have been narrowed down. If there is no penalty for it, a few more points can be added by wild guessing should a student not have time to answer all the questions.

CHAPTER SUMMARY

Just as there are strategies and techniques for studying for a test, there are strategies and techniques for taking a test. For an objective test, it is important that students learn to budget their exam time so they will be able to answer all the questions. The best way to answer all the questions is to do the easy ones the first time through, come back to the difficult ones the second time through (using cues to help decide on the answer), and then go through it one more time as a final check for careless errors.

Prepared students know how to look for inter-item cues—which are reliable informational cues—and for the probability cues of grammatical agreement qualifying and absolute words and word associations and synonyms. They also know about the cues specific to multiple-choice and matching questions.

Above all, they know the importance of reading the directions and the questions carefully and of being willing to guess, if there is no penalty for guessing, as a last resort.

A FINAL WORD

By now, it will have become clear that emphasizing preparedness is the best way to promote effective test taking among your students, adding to the mix familiarity with the right cues to use when their knowledge is incomplete. Students will find that the more they use these strategies of organization, preparation, and test taking, the better they will become at taking tests.

Let it be said that while knowing the subject is certainly very important, on a practical scale, it is not really enough. Students must also know how to take the different kinds of tests that will be used to sample their knowledge of a given subject. Being prepared is not a trick; it is having essential study skills—skills that make sense and are used by the most prepared, knowledgeable, and successful students.

Resources

Appendix A: A *Preparing Students* Final Test, Answers to Test Prep Exercises, and Answers to Final Test

Appendix B: Forms for Test Preparation and Study

Appendix C: Resources for Additional Test Preparation Assistance

Appendix D: Glossary

Appendix A

A *Preparing Students* Final Test, Answers to Test Prep Exercises, and Answers to Final Test

Now that your students have finished working through the information and exercises in this book, they should be on their way to becoming *prepared*. All it takes is practice, and you'll continue to give them plenty of opportunities for that!

To give them a chance to see how *prepared* they are and whether there are any points you should review with them, here's one final exercise. You can set your own time for giving this test (you can even use it to practice making a test-taking schedule, if you like). Each answer is worth one point. Note that many questions have more than one answer; for example, each match and each item in a list count as one answer and are worth one point. A total of 100 points is possible with no penalty for guessing. After students finish, work with them to compare their answers with the correct answers given after the test and have them count their points.

If more practice is needed in any particular area, or in the content covered in any particular chapter, use the material for your next test to provide more practice opportunities where and as needed.

You have taken the necessary steps for *Preparing Students for Testing and Doing Better in School* and are to be congratulated! No matter where your students are in their school careers, they will do better and be better prepared thanks to your work and efforts.

A *Preparing Students* Final Test

Part One: Doing Better in School

Chapter 1. How to Avoid Test Panic

1. Anxiety about tests
   A. can be desirable.
   B. is normal.
   C. can be excessive.
   D. is all of the above.
   E. is none of the above.

Answer: _____

2. To psych yourself up for a test, you need to think about how it relates to your _____.

3. Which of the following should you *not* do when preparing for a test?
   A. Allow yourself some quiet leisure time.
   B. Get a normal amount of sleep every night.
   C. Avoid physical activity.
   D. Reward yourself for hard work.
   E. Do all of the above.

Answer: _____

4. It is advisable to stay up all night just before a test but not to finish a paper.
   True _____ False _____ If false, underline the word or words that make it so.

5. Describe three relaxation techniques.
   (1)_____
   _____
   _____
   (2)_____
   _____
   _____
   (3)_____

6. To build a thorough set of notes, you should never
   A. use abbreviations and symbols.
   B. copy someone's notes if you've been absent.
   C. fill in gaps in your notes the same day of the class.
   D. record your teacher's examples exactly.
   E. None of the above

Answer: _____

7. To read a textbook chapter step by step, you should (1) look at the pictures, tables, and charts; (2) read the _____ ; (3) read the bold print; (4) read the _____ ; (5) read the questions or discussion points; (6) _____ ; (7) read the chapter text; and, if there's time, (8) _____ .

Chapter 2. How to Develop a Game Plan

8. On a master test schedule, you should indicate
   A. dates of tests.
   B. contents of tests.
   C. course names.
   D. midterms and finals.
   E. all of the above.

Answer: _____

9. A test analysis form helps you predict the format, time, and content of a test.
   True _____ False _____ If false, underline the word or words that make it so.

10. You should use old tests, when the teacher or counselor has made them available to you, to identify your general strengths and weaknesses and to memorize the answers.
    True _____ False _____ If false, underline the word or words that make it so.

11. What three questions do you need to answer to plan a study schedule for a test?

    (1) _____

    (2) _____

    (3) _____

12. To plan your study schedule for a test, you need to
    A. find time to finish all reading and assignments.
    B. set priorities.
    C. assign every free hour to study.
    D. do all of the above.
    E. do none of the above.

Answer: _____

13. The most important thing to do the day and night before an exam is to _____ and _____ the material.

14. To study for midterms and finals, you should allow yourself
    A. the entire term.
    B. two to three weeks.
    C. one to two weeks.
    D. four days.
    E. one week.

Answer: _____

15. Your game plan for studying for a test should include
    A. a master test schedule.
    B. a test analysis form.
    C. a study schedule for two weeks.
    D. daily lists of things to do.
    E. all of the above.

Answer: _____

Part Two: Preparing for All Tests

Chapter 3. Strategies for Test Study

16. An essay test requires recognition memory.
    True _____ False _____ If false, underline the word or words that make it so.

17. List three resources from which to make study notes in addition to your test analysis form.

    (1) _____

    (2) _____

    (3) _____

18. It is best to recite and memorize
    A. your readings.
    B. your class notes.
    C. your test analysis form.
    D. your condensed study notes.
    E. none of the above.

Answer: _____

19. Match the memorization technique with the kind of information to be memorized. Some techniques apply to more than one kind of information.

    _____ 1. Association   A. Poem
    _____ 2. Mnemonic connection B. Word definitions
    _____ 3. Whole learning   C. Speech
                                    D. Words in a specific order
                                    E. Multiword title

20. Because physical activity helps to promote recall, you should _____ and _____ information to be memorized.

21. Cramming is rote repetition, review, and reciting done just before a test.
    True_____ False _____ If false, underline the word or words that make it so.

Chapter 4. Preparing for Essay Questions and Tests

22. Predicting essay questions helps you
    A. actively think about the material.
    B. decide what information to memorize.
    C. practice essay answers.
    D. do all of the above.
    E. do none of the above.

Answer: _____

23. Match the kind of notes to the kind of essay question that is likely to be asked from them.

    _____ 1. A list of people or things   A. Long-answer trace question

    _____ 2. Steps of a process or historical development   B. Long-answer discussion question

    _____ 3. Descriptions of two or more things   C. Long-answer compare-and-contrast question

    _____ 4. Specific individual, situation, or institution   D. Short-answer question

24. To research topics, you can refer to
    A. online guides and indexes.
    B. the *Readers' Guide to Periodical Literature*.
    C. the current *Statistical Abstract of the United States*.
    D. B and C above.
    E. all of the above.

Answer: _____

25. When practicing answers for your essay questions, you should start by turning the questions into statements.

    True _____ False _____ If false, underline the word or words that make it so.

Chapter 5. Preparing for Objective Questions and Tests

26. An objective test requires recognition memory.

    True _____ False _____ If false, underline the word or words that make it so.

27. Match the descriptions with the type of objective questions.
    _____ 1. Multiple choice   A. A statement with a blank
    _____ 2. Matching   B. A stem and three to five alternatives
    _____ 3. True/false   C. Two columns
    _____ 4. Completion   D. A statement

28. Students who prepare for objective tests as thoroughly as for essay tests usually score higher than students who prepare only enough to recognize the correct answers.
True _____ False _____ Why?_____
_____

Part Three: Taking Tests and Doing Better

Chapter 6. Getting It Together on Test Day

29. You should try to arrive at the test room about 15 minutes early. List three things you should do during that time.
(1) _____
(2) _____
(3) _____

30. There are several things you should do before you start. One of them is to jot down memorized facts.
True _____ False _____ Why?_____
_____

31. It is also very important to listen to all directions your teacher gives you.
True _____ False _____ Why?_____
_____

32. If you are right-handed, put the exam on the right side of the desk and the answer sheet on the left.
True _____ False _____ If false, underline the word or words that make it so.

Chapter 7. Taking the Essay Test

33. You should always spend the same amount of time on every essay test question no matter how many points it is worth.
True _____ False _____ If false, underline the word or words that make it so.

34. List the four tasks to allot time for in your essay test schedule.
(1) _____
(2) _____
(3) _____
(4) _____

35. To give logical order to your essay, you should _____ it first.

36. The opening statement of an essay answer should restate the question.
True _____ False _____ If false, underline the word or words that make it so.

37. A deductive pattern in an essay means going from the main idea to the details. True _____ False _____ If false, underline the word or words that make it so.

38. You should always try to provide specific dates and numbers in your essay answers.
True _____ False _____ If false, underline the word or words that make it so.

Chapter 8. Taking the Objective Test

39. Match the appropriate amount of time with each step of taking an objective test that is 55 minutes long and has 50 questions worth an equal amount of points.

    _____ 1. Read directions and   A. 5 minutes
              plan schedule

    _____ 2. First go-through   B. 20 minutes

    _____ 3. Second go-through   C. 25 minutes

    _____ 4. Final check

40. On your first go-through, you should
    A. answer only the easier questions.
    B. answer every question.
    C. mark questions you're unsure of.
    D. do A and C.
    E. do none of the above.

Answer: _____

41. List three ways to try to figure out difficult questions on your second go-through.

    (1) _____

    (2) _____

    (3) _____

42. Match the types of questions in Column 2 to the appropriate test-question cues in Column 1. Some questions can be matched to more than one cue. (Hint: There are a total of 11 possible matches.)

    Column 1   *Column 2*

    _____ 1. Inter-item cue   A. Multiple choice

    _____ 2. Qualifying and absolute   B. Matching
              words

    _____ 3. Grammatical agreement   C. True/false

    _____ 4. Synonyms   D. Completion

43. A good strategy for answering multiple-choice questions is to try to
   A. anticipate the answers.
   B. eliminate alternatives.
   C. use cues.
   D. do all of the above.
   E. do none of the above.

Answer: _____

44. If you don't know an answer, you should always guess.
   True _____ False _____ Why?_____
   _____

45. If there is no penalty for guessing, you should always answer each question, even if you have to guess.
   True _____ False _____ Why?_____
   _____

Total Possible Points = 100

Your Total Test Score = _____

Test Prep Exercises: Answers

The answers here are only for those exercises for which the right answers can be expressed in only one way. Because the answers will vary for practice essays, no answers are provided here for those Test Prep exercises.

Exercise 2.1

1. 9/26

2. English

3. Vocabulary

4. No

5. English, Math, Psychology

6. (a) English and Math
   (b) Math, because it is a midterm test while the English test is only a weekly vocabulary test.

7. English, then Biology

8. Vocabulary or English; no

9. Week 2: Math, Chapters 1–3
   Week 3: Psychology, Unit 1
   Week 4: Math, Chapters 4–6
   Week 7: Math, Chapters 7–9
   Week 8: Psychology, Unit 3
   Week 9: Math, Chapters 10–12
   Although these tests are not as big as a midterm or final, all of them are bigger than a weekly vocabulary test and would probably be a larger percentage of the grade than a weekly test.

10. (a) Biology, Math, English, Psychology
    (b) English and Psychology
    (c) Biology and Math

Exercise 2.2

1. Textbook, class notes

2. No

3. (a) What is psychology, and how is it different from psychiatry? Relate the history of psychology and describe the four schools of psychology.
   (b) Each of these two areas will count 30 percent, while each of the other two will only count 20 percent.
   (c) Long-answer essays

(d)   Yes, because these two areas make up 60 percent of the test and the other areas make up only 40 percent of the test.

4. Yes:
definitions of major fields of psychology, definitions of the methods of psychology, the four schools of psychology, names and relative time periods from the history of psychology

5. Yes

Exercise 3.1

Harry's Psychology Class Notes

3   Abnormal Psych.—Studies all forms of abnormal human behavior.

3   Clinical Psych.—Deals with normal and abnormal behavior and with indiv. psychol. adjustment to oneself and one's environment.

3   Comparative Psych.—Studies behavior and abilities of different animal species.

3   Developmental Psych.—Studies changes in human behavior from birth to old age.

3   Educational Psych.—Applies the principles of psych. to the ed. process.

1   Psychology is the science that studies why human beings and animals behave as they do. The psychologist is interested in understanding the whole range of human experience.

1   Psychology is one of the behavioral sciences, like biology, sociology, and anthropology.

1   Psychiatry is a medical science dealing mostly with mental illness. Psychology studies all kinds of behavior, normal as well as abnormal. Psychiatrists are physicians with MD degrees and special training in the field of mental illness. Most psychologists have PhD or MA degrees instead of medical school training.

4   1.   Experiments—The experimental method enables a psychologist to control the conditions that determine the aspect of behavior being studied.

4   2.   Natural observation—The direct observation of human behavior in its natural environment

4   3.   Case histories—Collection of info about an individual's past and present life

4   4.   Surveys—The psychol. interviews members of a group by written questionnaires or orally. The psychol. can pull the info together and draw conclusions about average attitudes or behavior.

N/A   Psychological problems are often categorized by these terms: 1. neurosis, 2. psychosis, 3. paranoia, 4. schizophrenia, and 5. depression.

2   Behaviorism—Watson's (1913) reaction against structuralism. Watson called for the study of the observable behavior of humans and animals—not of their experiences.

2   Gestalt psychology—concerned with the organization of mental processes—we perceive organized patterns and the whole—Wertheimer, Kohier, Koffka, Lewin.

2   Psychoanalysis—Freud (early 1900s) developed a theory to explain why people become emotionally disturbed—people repress the needs and desires that are unacceptable to themselves or society.

N/A   Careers in psychology—For info, write Amer. Psych. Assoc., 750 First Street NW, Washington, DC 20002–4242.

3   Industrial psych.—Applies psych. principles and techniques to the needs and problems of industry.

3   Physiological psych.—Concerned with relationship between behavior and the function of the nervous system.

3   Social psych.—Studies relationships among people in groups and the formation of public opinion.

3   Personality studies—Studies the diff. characteristics of people and how these characteristics develop and can be measured.

3   Perception studies—Studies the process by which patterns of environmental energies become known as objects, events, people, and other aspects of the world.

2   Structuralism—Wundt—Thought main purpose of psych. was to describe and analyze conscious experience, including sensations, images, and feelings of which only the person himself is aware.

Exercise 4.1

(Wording may vary slightly.)

1. List the ways that a semicolon can be used.

2. List the ways that a comma can be used.

3. Name the main characters in *Gone With the Wind* and identify their traits.

4. Identify three late-19th-century American authors and list their works.

Exercise 4.2

(Wording may vary slightly.)

1. Trace the distribution of product from the manufacturer.

2. Trace the events leading to the Great Depression.

3. Describe the steps in warming up before exercising.

Exercise 4.3

(Wording may vary slightly.)

1. Compare and contrast the three main characters in Ken Kesey's *One Flew Over the Cuckoo's Nest*.

2. Compare and contrast the great American art forms and works of Georgia O'Keeffe, Louis Tiffany, and Frank Lloyd Wright.

3. Compare and contrast lines of longitude and lines of latitude.

Exercise 4.4

(Wording may vary slightly.)

1. Discuss the roles of the Olympians in Greek mythology.

2. Discuss the effects of the bombings of Hiroshima and Nagasaki.

3. Discuss the significance of the Jim Crow laws in the segregationist and civil rights movements.

Exercise 7.1

1. contrast

2. analyze, criticize, evaluate, review

3. describe or trace

4. give an example or illustrate

5. summarize or relate

6. describe or outline

7. analyze, discuss, or review

8. enumerate, list, name, describe, or outline

9. define or explain

10. compare, relate, or analyze

11. summarize, compare and contrast

12. summarize, describe, outline

Exercise 7.2

(Wording may vary slightly.)

1. *Exam Term(s):* identify. *Subject:* three late-19th-century American authors and their works. *Opening Statement:* Three late-19th-century American authors were Samuel Clemens (or Mark Twain), Edith Wharton, and Henry James.

2. *Exam Term(s):* describe. *Subject:* steps in formation of RNA. *Opening Statement:* RNA is formed by the following steps.

3. *Exam Term(s):* trace. *Subject:* events leading to the Revolutionary War in America. *Opening Statement:* The following important events led to the Revolutionary War in America.

4. *Exam Term(s):* compare and contrast. *Subject:* art forms and works of Georgia O'Keeffe, Louis Tiffany, and Frank Lloyd Wright. *Opening Statement:* The great American art forms and works of Georgia O'Keeffe, Louis Tiffany, and Frank Lloyd Wright include the following.

5. *Exam Term(s):* discuss. *Subject:* effects of Civil War in America. *Opening Statement:* Some of the effects of the Civil War in America were the following.

6. *Exam Term(s):* discuss. *Subject:* math and geography, lines of longitude and latitude. *Opening Statement:* Lines of longitude and lines of latitude have several important similarities and differences.

Exercise 8.1

1.	T	11.	T	21.	T	31.	T	41.	T
2.	T	12.	T	22.	T	32.	T	42.	T
3.	F	13.	T	23.	T	33.	T	43.	F
4.	T	14.	T	24.	T	34.	F	44.	F
5.	F	15.	F	25.	T	35.	F	45.	F
6.	F	16.	T	26.	F	36.	T	46.	T
7.	T	17.	T	27.	T	37.	F	47.	T
8.	F	18.	F	28.	F	38.	F	48.	T
9.	F	19.	T	29.	F	39.	F	49.	T
10.	F	20.	F	30.	F	40.	T	50.	F

Exercise 8.2

1.	B	11.	C	21.	B	31.	C	41.	B
2.	C	12.	C	22.	D	32.	C	42.	B
3.	C	13.	D	23.	C	33.	C	43.	C
4.	A	14.	B	24.	D	34.	B	44.	D
5.	B	15.	C	25.	B	35.	D	45.	C
6.	C	16.	C	26.	A	36.	B	46.	C
7.	D	17.	B	27.	C	37.	A	47.	A
8.	D	18.	A	28.	C	38.	C	48.	B
9.	A	19.	B	29.	D	39.	C	49.	D
10.	B	20.	C	30.	A	40.	D	50.	D

A *Preparing Students* Final Test: Answers

The total number of points you can get is 100. As you compare your answers with those that follow, note your score for each question in the blank beside the point value. (Each *part* of your answer is worth *one* point.) Then add up your score and transfer it to your test paper to see how prepared you've become in each area tested. If you missed questions, you can go back to the appropriate chapter sections and Test Prep exercises for a refresher.

_____ (1 pt.)   1. D

_____ (1 pt.)   2. ultimate goal in life

_____ (1 pt.)   3. C

_____ (2 pt.)   4. False, <u>all night</u>

_____ (3 pt.)   5. (three of the following four)
   (1) Inhale deeply with your eyes closed, hold your breath, and then exhale slowly.
   (2) Sit back in your chair, loosen your entire body, and close your eyes for a few minutes.
   (3) Tighten all your muscles, hold them, and then let them all loosen.
   (4) Tighten your muscles and then systematically loosen each one, one at a time.

_____ (1 pt.)   6. E

_____ (4 pt.)   7. (2) introduction
   (4) summary
   (6) skim
   (8) take notes

_____ (1 pt.)   8. E

_____ (2 pt.)   9. True. Because the statement is true, no words should be underlined.

_____ (2 pt.) 10. False, <u>and to memorize the answers</u>

_____ (3 pt.) 11. (1) How much time is available to study?
   (2) How good a grade do I need?
   (3) How much time will I need to study?

_____ (1 pt.) 12. B

_____ (2 pt.) 13. review, recite

_____ (1 pt.) 14. B

_____ (1 pt.) 15. E

_____ (2 pt.) 16. False, <u>recognition</u>

_____ (3 pt.) 17. (three of any of the following)
class notes, textbooks, library materials, handouts, lab notes, assignments

_____ (1 pt.) 18. D

_____ (5 pt.) 19. (1) B
(2) D, E
(3) A, C

_____ (2 pt.) 20. recite, write

_____ (2 pt.) 21. True. Because the statement is true, no words should be underlined.

_____ (1 pt.) 22. D

_____ (4 pt.) 23. (1) D
(2) A
(3) C
(4) B

_____ (1 pt.) 24. D

_____ (2 pt.) 25. True. Because the statement is true, no words should be underlined.

_____ (2 pt.) 26. True. Because the statement is true, no words should be underlined.

_____ (4 pt.) 27. (1) B
(2) C
(3) D
(4) A

_____ (2 pt.) 28. True. Because they have a more thorough knowledge of the material.

_____ (3 pt.) 29. (three of the following four)
(1) Review and recite memorized notes.
(2) Find a comfortable seat.
(3) Organize your materials.
(4) Practice relaxation techniques.

_____ (2 pt.) 30. True. So you will not risk forgetting these facts while you look over questions and begin to answer them.

_____ (2 pt.) 31. True. It is important to understand all directions before starting the test.

_____ (2 pt.) 32. False, <u>right side of the desk and the answer sheet on the left</u>

_____ (2 pt.) 33. False, <u>always</u> and/or <u>no matter how many points it is worth</u>

_____ (4 pt.) 34. (1) assessment and scheduling
(2) answering questions
(3) re-reading and finishing answers
(4) final checking

_____ (1 pt.) 35. outline

_____ (1 pt.) 36. rephrase

_____ (2 pt.) 37. True. Because the statement is true, no words should be underlined.

_____ (1 pt.) 38. False, <u>always</u> and/or <u>specific dates and numbers</u>

_____ (4 pt.) 39. (1) A
(2) C
(3) B
(4) A

_____ (1 pt.) 40. D

_____ (3 pt.) 41. (three of the following six)
(1) Re-read the directions and the question.
(2) Underline key words in the question.
(3) Ask the teacher to clarify the question.
(4) Reason through the question.
(5) Try to recall class lectures.
(6) Look for cues.

_____ (11 pt.) 42. (1) A, B, C, D
(2) A, C
(3) A, B, D
(4) A, B

_____ (1 pt.) 43. D

_____ (2 pt.) 44. False. There may be a penalty for guessing.

_____ (2 pt.) 45. True. You have nothing to lose by guessing if there is no penalty. If you don't answer questions, you signal to the teacher that you know nothing about those questions, but if you can narrow the alternatives and then guess a few answers correctly, you will get some credit.

_____ Your Total Test Score

Appendix B

Forms for
Test Preparation and Study

Master Test Schedule for Term
(Chapter 2)

Test Dates & Content	Course Names					
Week 1						
Week 2						
Week 3						
Week 4						
Week 5						
Week 6						
Week 7						
Week 8						
Week 9						
Week 10						
Week 11						
Week 12						
Week 13						
Week 14						
Week 15						
Week 16						
Finals Week						

Planning for Each Test (Chapter 2)

Name:_____

Date:_____

Class:_____

1. What do I already know about the topics?
   _____
   _____

2. What don't I know about the topics?
   _____
   _____

3. What clarifications do I need from my teacher?
   _____
   _____

4. What materials do I need to assemble to study?
   _____
   _____

5. What outside research do I need to do?
   _____
   _____

6. What reading do I still need to do?
   _____
   _____

7. What information seems most important?
   _____
   _____

8. How much time should I allow to prepare adequately for each area?
   _____
   _____

9. How much time do I actually have?
   _____
   _____

10. What is my game plan?
    _____
    _____

Test Analysis for Individual Tests (Chapter 2)

Class _____ Teacher _____

Date of Test _____ Time of Day _____

% of Grade _____ Major or Minor Test _____

What is the *format* of the test?		
Essay:		Long-Answer (discuss, trace, compare-and-contrast)
		Short-Answer (list, name, define, identify)
Objective:		True-False
		Multiple-Choice
		Matching
		Completion (fill-in-the-blank)

How many questions will be on the test? _____

How many of each kind of question will be on it?

	Long-Answer Essay		True/False
	Short-Answer Essay		Multiple-Choice
	Matching		Completion

How much time will I have for the test? _____

What is the *content* of the test?

Topics or Kinds of Problems	Sources of Content (notes, readings, labs)	Format of Questions*	% of Score and # of Questions

_____

_____

_____

_____

Are details or general concepts important?

_____

Do I have to know formulas or theorems? _____ If so, which ones?*

Do I have to know definitions? _____ If so, which ones?*_____

_____

Do I have to know important names and dates? _____ If so, which ones?* _____

_____

_____

_____

Will points be taken off for spelling errors?

_____

Can I bring a dictionary to use during the test?

_____

Can I bring a calculator to use during the test?

_____

If problems have to be worked out, how much credit is given for accuracy?
_____ and how much credit is given for method?

_____

Will this be an open-book test? _____

Are copies of previous exams available for inspection?

_____

Is this a departmental test or one made up by the teacher?

_____

Who will grade this test?**

_____

Do the writer and grader of this test have any special biases?**

_____

_____

Additional Clues or Notes:**

Notes:

*You may not be able to find this out before the test.

** You shouldn't ask this question of the teacher.

Study Schedule Questions (Chapter 2)

Name:_____

Date:_____

Class:_____

1. How much time is available to study for this test?

   _____

   _____

   _____

2. Where do I stand now in the class and how important is the test? How good a grade do I need on this test?

   _____

   _____

   _____

3. How much time does the test analysis form indicate that I will need to study adequately for the test?

   _____

   _____

   _____

Schedule (Chapter 2)

Two Weeks Before _____ Test

AM

	Mon.	Tues.	Wed.	Thurs.	Fri.	Sat.	Sun.
12–1							
1–2							
2–3							
3–4							
4–5							
5–6							
6–7							
7–8							
8–9							
9–10							
10–11							
11–12							

PM

12–1							
1–2							
2–3							
3–4							
4–5							
5–6							
6–7							
7–8							
8–9							
9–10							
10–11							
11–12							

Schedule (Chapter 2)

Week Before _____ Test

	Mon.	Tues.	Wed.	Thurs.	Fri.	Sat.	Sun.
AM							
12–1							
1–2							
2–3							
3–4							
4–5							
5–6							
6–7							
7–8							
8–9							
9–10							
10–11							
11–12							
PM							
12–1							
1–2							
2–3							
3–4							
4–5							
5–6							
6–7							
7–8							
8–9							
9–10							
10–11							
11–12							

Schedule (Chapter 2)

Week of _____ Test

	Mon.	Tues.	Wed.	Thurs.	Fri.	Sat.	Sun.
AM							
12–1							
1–2							
2–3							
3–4							
4–5							
5–6							
6–7							
7–8							
8–9							
9–10							
10–11							
11–12							

	Mon.	Tues.	Wed.	Thurs.	Fri.	Sat.	Sun.
PM							
12–1							
1–2							
2–3							
3–4							
4–5							
5–6							
6–7							
7–8							
8–9							
9–10							
10–11							
11–12							

Things-to-Do List (Chapter 2)

**Things to Do
to Study For** _____ **Test**   **Day or Date** _____ **Time** _____

Your First Daily List (Chapter 2)

Game Plan Checklist (Chapter 2)

To make sure your game plan for studying for each test is complete, check off the items in this list as you get them done.

_____ 1. Did I prepare a *master test schedule* for the term, putting in all the dates?

_____ 2. Did I cross out all my fixed commitments on the *schedules for one week before the test and the week of the test* (two weeks before midterm and final tests) and note when I have other tests during those weeks?

_____ 3. Did I figure out when I have *study time available* on these schedules for each test?

_____ 4. Did I prepare a *test analysis form* using information from class, from the teacher, and from other sources?

_____ 5. Have I checked to see if *past exams* are available for review?

_____ 6. Using my test analysis form and past exams (if they were available to me), did I determine the *format of the test* so I know whether to prepare for objective or essay questions?

_____ 7. Using my test analysis form, did I assess *where I am right now in terms of reading* and other assignments related to the test?

_____ 8. Did I make a complete *list of things to do* to prepare for the test, putting the most important items first and planning when to do them according to the time available on my study schedule?

_____ 9. Am I going to break down the things-to-do list into *daily lists* on cards?

Once you have checked off all the items on the list, you are ready for the next step—preparing and studying for your test!

Short-Answer Questions (Chapter 4)

Name:_____

Date:_____

Class:_____

1. Predicted short-answer question:

_____

_____

_____

Predicted answer:

_____

_____

_____

2. Predicted short-answer question:

_____

_____

_____

Predicted answer:

_____

_____

_____

3. Predicted short-answer question:

_____

_____

_____

Predicted answer:

_____

_____

_____

4. Predicted short-answer question:

_____

_____

_____

Predicted answer:

_____

_____

_____

_____

Long-Answer Trace Questions (Chapter 4)

Name:_____

Date:_____

Class:_____

1. Predicted long-answer question:

_____

_____

_____

Predicted answer:

_____

_____

_____

2. Predicted long-answer question:

_____

_____

_____

Predicted answer:

_____

_____

_____

3. Predicted long-answer question:

_____

_____

_____

Predicted answer:

_____

_____

_____

Long-Answer Compare-and-Contrast Trace Questions (Chapter 4)

Name:_____

Date:_____

Class:_____

1. Predicted long-answer question:

_____

_____

_____

Predicted answer:

_____

_____

_____

2. Predicted long-answer question:

_____

_____

_____

Predicted answer:

_____

_____

_____

3. Predicted long-answer question:

_____

_____

_____

Predicted answer:

_____

_____

_____

Long-Answer Discussion Questions (Chapter 4)

Name:_____

Date:_____

Class:_____

1. Predicted long-answer question:

_____

_____

_____

Predicted answer:

_____

_____

_____

2. Predicted long-answer question:

_____

_____

_____

Predicted answer:

_____

_____

_____

3. Predicted long-answer question:

_____

_____

_____

Predicted answer:

_____

_____

_____

Researching a Topic (Chapter 4)

Name:_____

Date:_____

Class:_____

Choose a topic to research: _____

_____

_____

_____

Research the topic or person on programs available on your library's computers or in appropriate printed indexes.

Name of Periodical	Name of Article	Author	Date	Volume	Pages
1.					
2.					
3.					

Find one of the articles listed above, and skim for two or three important facts.

1.

_____

_____

2.

_____

_____

3.

_____

_____

Researching Statistics (Chapter 4)

Name:_____

Date:_____

Class:_____

Choose a topic to research:_____

_____

_____

_____

_____

Use the current *Statistical Abstract of the United States* or find even more up-to-date statistics by using an online resource. Look up your topic and cite three statistics relevant to your topic.

Statistic   Source, or Survey Done By   Date

1. _____

2. _____

3. _____

Researching a Famous Person (Chapter 4)

Name:_____

Date:_____

Class:_____

Choose a famous person to research: _____

_____

_____

_____

Use *Current Biography* or another biographical resource, electronic or print. Find three sources in one of these indexes and provide the information below.

Name of Book or Periodical   Name of Article   Author   Date   Volume   Pages

1. _____

2. _____

3. _____

Find one of the articles listed above and skim it for two or three important facts.

1.

_____

_____

2.

_____

_____

3.

_____

_____

Multiple-Choice Questions (Chapter 5)

Name:_____

Date:_____

Class:_____

1. Stem:

_____

_____

A. _____

B. _____

C. _____

D. _____

Answer: _____

2. Stem:

_____

_____

A. _____

B. _____

C. _____

D. _____

Answer: _____

3. Stem:

_____

_____

A. _____

B. _____

C. _____

D. _____

Answer: _____

Matching Questions (Chapter 5)

Name:_____

Date:_____

Class:_____

1. Question:

_____

- -

_____   _____

_____   _____

_____   _____

_____   _____

_____   _____

Answer: _____

2. Question:

_____

- -

_____   _____

_____   _____

_____   _____

_____   _____

_____   _____

Answer: _____

3. Question:

_____

- -

_____   _____

_____   _____

_____   _____

_____   _____

_____   _____

Answer: _____

True/False Questions (Chapter 5)

Name:_____

Date:_____

Class:_____

1. Question:

_____

_____

Answer:_____

_____

_____

2. Question:

_____

_____

Answer:_____

_____

_____

3. Question:

_____

_____

Answer:_____

_____

_____

4. Question:

_____

_____

Answer:_____

_____

_____

Completion Questions (Chapter 5)

Name:_____

Date:_____

Class:_____

1. Question:

_____

_____

Answer:_____

_____

_____

2. Question:

_____

_____

Answer:_____

_____

_____

3. Question:

_____

_____

Answer:_____

_____

_____

4. Question:

_____

_____

Answer:_____

_____

_____

The Opening Statement (Chapter 7)

Name:_____

Date:_____

Class:_____

1. Predicted Essay Question:

_____

_____

Exam Terms:

_____

Subject of Question:

_____

Opening Statement:

_____

2. Predicted Essay Question:

_____

_____

Exam Terms:

_____

Subject of Question:

_____

Opening Statement:

_____

3. Predicted Essay Question:

_____

_____

Exam Terms:

_____

Subject of Question:

_____

Opening Statement:

_____

4. Predicted Essay Question:

_____

_____

Exam Terms:

_____

Subject of Question:

_____

Opening Statement:

_____

_____

Appendix C

Resources for Additional Test Preparation Assistance

WEB SITES

Following is a list of Web sites addressing test preparation that may be of further use to teachers, students, and parents. Many of these links are to college and university Web sites that have wonderful tips, useful for students in middle school and high school as well as college. These links were last verified in August 2007.

www.testprepreview.com (Test Prep Review). Free information on preparing for various types of tests, including standardized tests

http://regentsprep.org (Oswego City School District, New York). Information on preparing for tests in various subjects

www.sdc.uwo.ca/learning/tentt.html (University of Western Ontario, Canada). Ten tips for success in school

www.rio.maricopa.edu/distance_learning/tutorials/study/learn.shtml (Rio Salado College Online, Arizona). Information on "Learning to Learn"

www.csun.edu/~hflrc006/51ways.html (California State University–Northridge). Information on "51 Ways to Better Your Grades"

www.geocities.com/Heartland/9120/learner.html (written by Ian Graham). Quiz to help students determine if they are effective learners

www.midtel.net/~natebg/parents.htm (written by Nate Becker). List of "Ways Parents Can Help" students

www.school-for-champions.com/grades.htm (School for Champions). List of "Strategies to Succeed in School"

www.ucc.vt.edu/stdysk/checklis.html (Virginia Polytechnic Institute and State University). "Study Skills Checklist"

www.sp.uconn.edu/~ph101vc/study/Improve.html (University of Connecticut). A good summary of ways to improve study skills and how to avoid the "Ten Traps of Studying"

http://studytips.aac.ohiou.edu (Ohio University). Information on many aspects of study skills, such as note taking, concentration, memory, and time management

www.wholefamily.com/aboutteensnow/homework_help/study_tips/from_teen.html (WholeFamily.com, written by Elie Klein). An article that teens may enjoy entitled "Study Tips From a Teen Who's Been There (And Even Made Valedictorian in the End)" containing ten tips for success in school

www.bmb.psu.edu/courses/psu16/troyan/studyskills/general.htm (Pennsylvania State University). General study tips

www.southwestern.edu/academic/acser-skills-teststr.html (Southwestern University, Texas). Many tips and strategies for studying for and taking various types of tests

www.frontiernet.net/~jlkeefer/exams.htm (Brockport High School, New York, adapted from material from Pennsylvania State University). Article instructing students how to study for exams

www.mzmarcotte.com/StudySkills.htm (Laurie Sproul Marcotte, educator). A good summary of how to prepare for a test or quiz

www.senri.ed.jp/Departments/english/tststd.htm (English Department, Osaka International School, Japan). Creative suggestions on how to study

http://all.successcenter.ohio-state.edu/all-tour/study-assistance.htm (Ohio State University). List of some study strategies and test preparation methods

www.open.ac.uk/skillsforstudy/ (The Open University, United Kingdom). Many resources related to success in school covering topics such as how to summarize, managing stress, learning styles, and giving presentations

www.ncsu.edu/felder-public/Columns/memo.html (Professor Richard M. Felder, North Carolina State University). An open memo to students who have been disappointed in their test scores with a checklist of how to study effectively

www.d.umn.edu/kmc/student/loon/acad/strat/test_take.html (University of Minnesota–Duluth). List of some test-taking strategies

www.bucks.edu/~specpop/tests.htm (Bucks County Community College, Pennsylvania). List of some test-taking strategies

www.cbv.ns.ca/sstudies/links/learn/stutips.html#3 (Kevin Kearney, educator, Breton Education Centre, Nova Scotia, Canada). Many study and test-taking tips

www.eiu.edu/~lrnasst/tests.htm (Eastern Illinois University). Information on taking various types of tests

http://childdevelopmentinfo.com/learning/studytips.shtml (Child Development Institute). Useful tips for parents and students

www.teachersandfamilies.com/open/studymatrix.html (Teachers and Families). Lengthy, well-organized database of links to topic-specific Web sites to assist K–12 students with their studies

BOOKS

Calkins, L., Montgomery, K., Santman, D., & Falk, B. (1998). *A teacher's guide to standardized reading tests: Knowledge is power.* Portsmouth, NH: Heinemann.

Capper, J. (1996). *Testing to learn: Learning to test.* Newark, DE: International Reading Association.

Chapman, C., & King, R. (2005). *Differentiated assessment strategies: One tool doesn't fit all.* Thousand Oaks, CA: Corwin Press.

Cizek, G. J., & Burg, S. S. (2006). *Addressing test anxiety in high-stakes environments.* Thousand Oaks, CA: Corwin Press.

Cole, A. D. (2003). *The process and the prompt, Book 1.* Portsmouth, NH: Heinemann.

Devine, T. G., & Kania, J. S. (2003). In J. Flood, D. Lapp, J. R. Squire, & J. M. Jensen (Eds.), *Handbook of research on teaching the English language arts* (2nd ed., pp. 942–954). Mahwah, NJ: Lawrence Erlbaum Associates.

Flippo, R. F. (2003). *Assessing readers: Qualitative diagnosis and instruction.* Portsmouth, NH: Heinemann.

Flippo, R. F. (2004). *Texts and tests: Teaching study skills across content areas.* Portsmouth, NH: Heinemann.

Glasgow, N. A., McNary, S. J., & Hicks, C. D. (2006). *What successful teachers do in diverse classrooms: 71 research-based classroom strategies for new and veteran teachers.* Thousand Oaks, CA: Corwin Press.

Greene, A. H., & Melton, G. D. (2007). *Test talk: Integrating test preparation into reading workshop.* Portland, ME: Stenhouse.

Weinstein, C. E., & Meyer, R. E. (1986). The teaching of learning strategies. In M. C. Whitrock (Ed.), *Handbook of research on teaching* (3rd ed., pp. 315–317). New York: Macmillan.

Wormeli, R. (2006). *Fair isn't always equal: Assessing & grading in the differentiated classroom.* Portland, ME: Stenhouse.

Appendix D

Glossary

GLOSSARY

absolute words: words such as *always, never, all,* or *nobody*

alternatives: all possible answers or statements to choose from in a multiple-choice question

analyze: long-answer essay term that signals the student to appraise a situation or problem, citing both advantages and limitations, and emphasizing one's personal evaluation in light of the appraisal of authorities

classify: short-answer essay term that signals the student to group information in a diagram, chart, or description according to its main parts or characteristics

compare: long-answer essay term that signals the student to emphasize the similarities between two (or more) things

compare-and-contrast question: long-answer essay question that requires the student to describe two or more things that have both similar and dissimilar characteristics

completion question: fill-in-the-blank question in which one must recall the answer rather than recognize it among a number of alternatives

content validity: validity determined based on how well the test covers and assesses content that has been studied by the students being tested

contrast: long-answer essay term that signals the student to stress the differences between two or more objects, ideas, qualities, characteristics, events, or concepts

cramming: the rote repetition, review, and reciting a student does just before an exam to keep the information freshly in mind

criterion-referenced test: a test in which the examinee's score is expressed in terms of how successfully the student met the objectives, or predetermined criteria, of the given test

criticize: long-answer essay term that signals the student to express judgment about the merit or truth of the factors, concepts, or views mentioned

cue: clue in a test question or format that may signal the correct answer

cut-off score: the predetermined passing score of a criterion-referenced test

defend: long-answer essay term that signals the student to present one side of an argument, issue, or situation

define: short-answer essay term that signals the student to give concise, clear, and authoritative meanings

describe: essay term that signals the student to recount or relate in sequence the step(s) requested

diagram: short-answer essay term that signals the student to make a drawing, chart, plan, or other graphic answer

discuss question: long-answer essay question that requires the student to describe a specific individual, situation, or institution

educated guessing: guessing at an answer after eliminating obviously wrong alternatives; the guessing done after having narrowed down the choices

enumerate: short-answer essay term that signals the student to write the relevant information in a list or in outline form

essay test: test that requires the student to have an overall understanding of content; often several variations of answers are acceptable; to answer requires recalling the important concepts and ideas and writing a short- or long-essay response

evaluate: long-answer essay term that signals the student to appraise a problem or situation, citing both advantages and limitations and emphasizing the appraisal of authorities and, to a lesser degree, one's personal appraisal

explain: long-answer essay term that signals the student to interpret, clarify, and carefully spell out the material

give an example: short-answer essay term that signals the student to cite one instance or situation to make a point

high-stakes test: another name for any standardized test that is used for very important purposes; for instance, entrance and/or exit requirements of schools, colleges, and special programs and requirements for graduation/promotion

illustrate: short-answer essay term that signals the student to use a picture, diagram, or concrete example to explain or clarify the answer

inter-item cue: a question in a test that provides information about the answer to another question

interpret: long-answer essay term that signals the student to translate, give examples of, solve, or comment on a subject

justify: long-answer essay term that signals the student to prove or give reasons for decisions or conclusions

list: short-answer essay term that signals the student to write an itemized series of concise statements giving names, things, or points one by one

long-term memory: memory that is internalized and stored in the brain for future recall

master test schedule: a complete schedule of all the tests the student needs to take for the entire term for all classes

matching question: question on an objective test that requires the student to match the stems (leads) from one list with the alternatives (possible answers) on another list

memorization: the rote repetition, review, and reciting done to instill knowledge in long-term memory

mnemonic connection: an artificial device or imaginary connection used to aid one's memory

multiple-choice question: question on an objective test that requires the student to choose one of three, four, or five possible answers

name: short-answer essay term that signals the student to make a list of important names or components

no penalty for guessing: describes a test whose score is based only on the number of correct answers and incorrect answers do not count more than unanswered questions

norm-referenced test: a test in which the examinee's score is expressed in terms of a comparison with how others scored on the same test

objective test: test that requires the student to recognize correct answers, often requiring knowledge of specific facts

outline: essay term that signals the student to organize an answer under main points and subordinate points, stressing the process or relationships among events or ideas

penalty for guessing: describes a test on which more points are taken off for incorrect answers than for unanswered questions

prove: long-answer essay term that signals the student to establish that something is true by citing factual evidence or giving clear, logical reasoning

qualifying words: words such as *generally, often, some,* or *most*

raw score: number of correct answers on a student's test

recall: the retrieval of stored information from the brain's memory

recognition: knowing the right information upon seeing it because one has seen it before

relate: long-answer essay term that signals the student to show how things are connected to each other or how one thing causes another, correlates with another, or is similar to another

resources: class notes, reading, and other assignments that can help a student study for a test

retention: remembering

review: long-answer essay term signaling the student to examine a subject critically and analyze and comment on important information about it

schedule: diagram or chart that allots specific times to specific tasks

short-term memory: fleeting and limited memory

skim: to look quickly at key words, sentences, and ideas in a text

standardized test: commercial test that is developed to assess one's knowledge of certain topics or subjects and is given under prescribed and uniform conditions

state: short-answer essay term that signals the student to present main points in a brief, clear sequence, usually omitting details, illustrations, and examples

stem: the lead or introduction part of a multiple-choice question

subjective test: test that requires the student to have an overall understanding of content; often several variations of answers are acceptable

summarize: short-answer essay term that signals the student to give the main points or facts in a condensed form, omitting minor details and examples

test analysis: the process of considering all information possible about a test

test-wise: knowing how to study for and successfully take the various required tests

time management: the process of deciding which tasks are most important and least important and then scheduling one's time accordingly

trace question: long-answer essay question that requires the student to outline or describe the steps of a process or the historical development of something

true/false question: a question on an objective test that requires the student to decide if a statement is right or wrong

whole learning: reviewing and learning material by thinking about how the material is interrelated

wild guessing: answering objective test questions without having any idea whether one's answer is correct or not; random guessing

References

Andriessen, I., Phalet, K., & Lens, W. (2006). Future goal setting, task motivation and learning of minority and non-minority students in Dutch school. *British Journal of Educational Psychology, 76*(4), 827–850.

Barbarick, K. A., & Ippolito, J. A. (2003). Does the number of hours studied affect exam performance? *Journal of Natural Resources and Life Sciences Education, 32*, 32–35.

Be a better test taker! (2002, September 3). *Scholastic News, 59*, S1–S20.

Bower, B. (2007). Sleep on it. *Science News, 171*(17), 260–261.

Brown, S. L., & Schiraldi, G. R. (2004). Reducing subclinical symptoms of anxiety and depressions: A comparison of two college courses. *American Journal of Health Education, 35*(3), 158–164.

Carlson, J. K., Hoffman, J., Gray, D., & Thompson, A. (2004). A musical interlude: Using music and relaxation to improve reading performance. *Intervention in School and Clinic, 39*(4), 246–250.

Casbarro, J. (2004). Reducing anxiety in the era of high-stakes testing. *Principal, 83*(5), 36–38.

Cifuentes, L., & Hsieh, Y. J. (2003). Visualization for construction of meaning during study time: A quantitative analysis. *International Journal of Instructional Media, 30*(3), 263–273.

Cukras, G. A. G. (2006). The investigation of study strategies that maximize learning for underprepared students. *College Teaching, 54*(1), 194–197.

Elliott, S. N., DiPerna, J. C., Mroch, A. A., & Lang, S. C. (2004). Prevalence and patterns of academic enabling behaviors: An analysis of teachers' and students' ratings for a national sample of students. *School Psychology Review, 33*(2), 302–309.

Flippo, R. F. (2002a). Standardized testing. In B. J. Guzzetti (Ed.), *Literacy in America: An encyclopedia of history, theory, and practice* (Vol. 2, pp. 615–617). Santa Barbara, CA: ABC-CLIO.

Flippo, R. F. (2002b). Test preparation. In B. J. Guzzetti (Ed.), *Literacy in America: An encyclopedia of history, theory, and practice* (Vol. 2, pp. 650–651). Santa Barbara, CA: ABC-CLIO.

Flippo, R. F., Becker, M. J., & Wark, D. C. (in press). Test taking. In R. F. Flippo & D. C. Caverly (Eds.), *Handbook of college reading and study strategy research* (2nd ed.). New York: Routledge/Taylor & Francis.

Flippo, R. F., & Schumm, J. S. (in press). Reading tests. In R. F. Flippo & D. C. Caverly (Eds.), *Handbook of college reading and study strategy research* (2nd ed.). New York: Routledge/Taylor & Francis.

Gabriele, A. (2007). The influence of achievement goals on the constructive activity of low achievers during collaborative problem solving. *British Journal of Educational Psychology, 77*(1), 121–141.

Gates, G. S. (2005). Awakening to school community: Buddhist philosophy for educational reform. *The Journal of Educational Thought, 39*(2), 140–173.

Gettinger, M., & Seibert, J. K. (2002). Contributions of study skills to academic competence. *School Psychology Review, 31*(3), 350–366.

Goodstein, M. (1999). Everyday study skills. *Instructor, 114*(2), 43–46, 48.

Johnson, G. M. (2006). Online study groups: Reciprocal peer questioning versus mnemonic devices. *Journal of Educational Computing Research, 35*(1), 83–96.

Kim, J. (2005). Memory upgrade. *Current Health 2, 32*(2), 20–43.

Klomegah, R. (2007). Predictors of academic performance of university students: An application of the goal efficacy model. *College Student Journal, 41*(2), 407–415.

Kobayashi, K. (2006). Combined effects of note-taking/-reviewing on learning and the enhancement through interventions: A meta-analytic review. *Educational Psychology, 26*(3), 459–477.

Kras, J. M., Strand, B. N., Abendroth-Smith, J., & Mathesius, P. (1999). Teaching study skills through classroom activities. *Journal of Physical Education, Recreation & Dance, 70*(1), 40–44.

Kuo, J., Hagie, C., & Miller, M. T. (2004). Encouraging college student success: The instructional challenges, response strategies, and study skills of contemporary undergraduates. *Journal of Instructional Psychology, 31*(1), 60–67.

Lester, D. (1991). Speed and performance on college course examinations. *Perceptual and Motor Skills, 73*(3), 1090.

Merrett, J., & Merrett, F. (1997). Correspondence training as a means of improving study skills. *Educational Psychology, 17*(4), 469–482.

Onwuegbuzie, A. J. (1994). Examination-taking strategies used by college students in statistics courses. *College Student Journal, 28*(2), 163–174.

Petress, K. C. (2004). The benefits of group study. *Education, 124*(4), 587–589.

Pikulski, J. J. (1990). The role of tests in a literacy assessment program. *The Reading Teacher, 43*(9), 686–688.

Stickgold, R., Hobson, J. A., Fosse, R., & Fosse, M. (2001). Sleep, learning, and dreams: Off-line memory reprocessing. *Science, 294*(5544), 1052–1057.

Supon, V. (2004). Implementing strategies to assist test-anxious students. *Journal of Instructional Psychology, 31*(4), 292–296.

Valencia, S. W., & Wixon, K. K. (2000). Policy-oriented research on literacy standards and assessment. In M. L. Kamil, P. B. Mosenthal, P. D. Pearson, & R. Barr (Eds.), *Handbook of reading research* (Vol. 3, pp. 909–935). Mahwah, NJ: Lawrence Erlbaum Associates.

Viadero, D. (2004). Researchers explorer ways to lower students' stress. *Education Week, 23*(38), 8.

Index